Two Happy Homes

*A Working Guide for
Parents & Stepparents
After
Divorce and Remarriage*

Shirley Thomas, Ph.D.

Two Happy Homes: A Working Guide for Parents & Stepparents After Divorce and Remarriage

Springboard Publications
P.O. Box 484
Longmont, Colorado 80502-0484

Illustrations: Holliday Thompson
Cover and Text Design: RankinFiles Communications
Edited by Dorothy Rankin

Library of Congress Control Number 2005900994

ISBN 0-9646378-0-4

www.parentsareforever.com

For Children Everywhere
Living In Two Homes

~~~~~~~~~~~~~~~~~~~~~~~~

I would like to express gratitude for the work of all
teachers, writers and researchers who have gone
before me in developing the knowledge and ideas
about families that led to the writing of this book.

Forward

THE DILEMMA OF THE CHILD

Every year millions of children are affected by divorce because their parents could not make their marriage last. Although the divorce rate is falling slightly, it still hovers near 50 percent, and at least 75 percent of separated women and men remarry. According to the U.S. Census Bureau 65 percent of these second marriages involve children of one, or both, parties.

The modern American family is forever changed from what it was fifty years ago, and there is no longer a "typical" family constellation. More than half of all children eventually live part time with one or both of their parents, and although the Census Bureau still counts only one primary home per child, millions of children live in two. By the year 2010 the number of stepfamily homes in this country will exceed both the number of single-parent households and conventional homes with two original parents.

In spite of these astounding statistics, as a practicing psychologist I still find that children want one family image. The family may grow and become extended as parents move on with their lives, but girls and boys are happiest when they can think of their families as somehow united. Even children who hang on to the common fantasy that their biological parents will some-day remarry express feelings of pleasure and well-being when their two homes are harmonious.

Over the past ten to fifteen years, various writers of self-help books for parents have emphasized the value of learning to cooperate in their parenting after divorce. A number of others have focused on the challenges faced by members of new step-families. Few books have emerged, however, that address the needs of newly divorced parents as they transition into remarriage. Fathers, mothers, and stepparents, often in the process of making different kinds of family adjustments simultaneously, need strategies for learning to parent across two households.

In *Two Happy Homes* I present a plan for divorced coparents and new stepparents to learn to work together. My hope is that it will help parents who read it come closer to attaining the kind of unity their children sorely long for. The book is organized sequentially, beginning with the process of divorce and taking readers through remarriage toward a positive restructuring of the larger family network. It will provide the most help to parents who read it completely from beginning to end, so moms and dads in different roles can understand each other's problems and develop an appreciation for the value of working together.

Table of Contents

Chapter 5 Empathy Helps and Heals

Chapter 6 Rulebook for the Family of Parents

Chapter 7 Bending, Flexing, and Building

Chapter 1

DIVORCE: ENDINGS AND BEGINNINGS

Parents Are Forever

When young women and men marry, they believe their love will last forever. Thinking the future will be wonderful, first-time spouses look forward to shaping their hopes and dreams together by working, acquiring homes, and having children. Only later, when nearly half of all married couples are faced with the reality of divorce, do they realize they will lose much of what they have built together.

This book is not about divorce per se, but rather about the emotional and practical changes it triggers in the life plans of fathers and mothers. If children were not a consequence of marital intimacy, this guide would not be necessary. Adults who are childless can literally move on when their relationship ends. But when innocent girls and boys are involved, there is no simple way out. Parenting is a continuing responsibility until the children are grown.

In my work with families, I have found that divorce does not necessarily cause everlasting emotional damage to children — but it can. There is such a thing as a good divorce, and certainly there are good second marriages. But there are also bad divorces and bad second marriages which hurt the children involved. What distinguishes good from bad in both is the quality of relationships between the adults and children and the maturity of each spouse, old and new, as a parent.

A profound feeling of loss sets in when we sense the inevitability of a pending separation.

The Process and Stages of Grief

From early childhood we learn that happiness results in part from acquisition. As we outgrow the "getting" of toys and playthings as youngsters, we later move on to getting education, careers, and families of our own. But when we sense the inevitability of a pending separation, a profound feeling of loss sets in. Because we are unaccustomed to losing rather than gaining things in life, feelings of emotional confusion and agitation always accompany the dismantling of a family unit.

In her works on death and dying, Elisabeth Kübler-Ross described grief as a process broken into stages. Divorce and separation cause grief in both spouses and the children because of the losses involved. The family as you knew it is gone, along with your hopes for the future.

The five stages of grief as related to divorce are:

1. *Denial: Lack of recognition of loss; a refusal to deal with reality.* Parents and children in denial will have

trouble talking or hearing about divorce, and will use this mechanism to cope.

2. *Anger: Resentment, blame, or frustration, usually directed outward.* Parents or children become highly emotional and upset when the reality of loss sets in.

3. *Bargaining: Unrealistic effort to delay divorce or reunite the family.* Spouses propose reconciliation and children fantasize that this will happen.

4. *Depression: Sadness felt when denial and anger subside and the finality of loss becomes inescapable.* Children and parents alike may shed tears, withdraw, or show other signs of depression.

5. *Acceptance: Awareness that life will go on after divorce.* Feelings of peace and well-being begin to overcome negative emotions, and happiness is restored.

Although divorce is technically just the end of a marriage contract, the losses it causes are multiple, including loss of the parenting contract as you know it and loss of being with your children every day. Parents who never married but were in a close relationship mourn their loss in much the same way. Separation feels like a promise has been broken, and grief is inevitable wherever there once was commitment. Grief is also at the root of the unbearable turmoil which so often accompanies divorce, because the experience is so traumatic.

The way in which grief is manifest will depend on the personality of each spouse and upon the situation, but anger is the

Separation feels like a promise has been broken, and grief is inevitable wherever there once was commitment.

most hurtful and devastating reaction. A few examples will illustrate how adult anger affects children:

- A spouse who was left for another man or woman feels hate for both the former spouse and the replacement, and says so, even to the children. "I despise your stupid mother and that awful man too."

- A partner finally free of a controlling, demanding spouse berates the former partner to others and to the children. "Your father is nothing but a control freak."

- A spouse who struggles financially keeps the children away from the other parent out of anger, spite and a need to punish. "My kids don't need a deadbeat parent."

Separated mothers and fathers fall into patterns of hurting each other repeatedly, almost purposely, just to stay connected.

Unfortunately, in each of these situations the grieving parent fails to consider the needs or feelings of the child and unwittingly inflicts harm. Verbally abusing your former partner, especially in front of your daughter or son, directly lowers your child's self-esteem because your child identifies strongly with both parents. It also creates conflict and confusion and makes the child's recovery from grief more difficult.

All parents love their children, but many hurt them when intense emotions cause their own conflicts to be acted out. Your children loved both of you when the family was together, and they will love you both apart, regardless of your opinion of the other parent. Learning to respect this basic right of all boys and girls by keeping negative feelings to yourself is a major responsibility for parting parents.

Moving Away from Intimacy

One key to getting past the problematic stage of anger is in recognizing the role of intimacy, during and after marriage. Married partners are more than friends because they share their innermost selves with one another, including their sexual and emotional selves. With the end of a marriage, no matter what the reason, the intimacy should also end, and parents need to restructure how they relate.

A common mistake happens when former partners who cannot bear the loss of daily contact cling to a dynamic we call *negative intimacy*. Here separated mothers and fathers fall into patterns of hurting each other repeatedly, almost purposely, just to stay connected. A close but negative bond sometimes feels better than no bond at all, and conflict serves the purpose of keeping spouses involved with each other.

Parents need to recognize that negative intimacy can be a factor in their post-divorce relationship and should learn other ways of getting their personal needs met. Later in this book I will suggest how new relationships can help, but first moving away from an original intimate partner, physically and emotionally, is central to the process of healing.

Emotional separation is the most important step in putting the needs of your children first. Parents who cling to negative intimacy are postponing their divorce recovery, making life in the future difficult for themselves and for the children.

The Task of Becoming Coparents

Instead of thinking about divorce as an ending, you should consider it the beginning of a new way of life.

The first step in achieving family happiness after surviving the pain of divorce is to accept your child's reality. Though you no longer live together, your children still love you both. In almost every case, both mothers and fathers should remain active with the children. Only in rare instances involving serious substance abuse, domestic violence, or debilitating mental illness is cooperative parenting impossible. All other parents are charged with learning to work together so the child's world will not become fragmented.

The task of revising the parenting relationship gets easier when both partners let go of intimacy, positive or negative, and begin to view each other with neutrality. Throughout this book, I present ideas that will give you a balanced perspective about yourself and your child's other parent. If you can develop a sense of empathy for your former spouse, for example, you will be less apt to project anger outward because you will better understand his or her behavior.

Coparenting effectively takes enormous amounts of strength and determination. Focusing on your own life when the children are with the other parent will help, as will other coping skills. One of these skills is *reframing*, which means looking at a situation differently, from another angle or perspective. Instead of thinking about divorce as an ending, for example, you should consider it the beginning of a new way of life. This will make accepting the idea of cooperating with your child's other parent more attractive, especially if you also think of it as a new start in life for your child.

Conflict between parents and households always hurts children caught in the middle. Arguing or fighting in front of boys and girls not only demonstrates poor problem-solving, but can be quite frightening to a child. At the time of separation and for some time after, parent emotions are high, and harmful eruptions of anger may occur. Loving coparents should learn to recognize conflict escalation as a danger sign in the family and strive to manage their grief better.

The Coparent Business Relationship

The most peaceful working model for coparents to follow is one of the business relationship. Because they are no longer intimates or lovers, even the concept of friendship usually carries too much closeness for divorced parents to relate in a successful way. Isolina Ricci first wrote about the idea of separated parents becoming business partners in *Mom's House, Dad's House*. Now most experts recommend the model of the business partnership as the best plan for divorced and never-married parents to use as they learn how to work together.

Put simply, coparents are partners in the business of rearing the children they had together. When the legal divorce is complete, parents are required by the state to file parenting plans on behalf of the children. You should think of this plan as a business contract you enter into freely. Specific items in the contract are commitments you both make for your son or daughter, and they are promises you should keep.

To develop the best parenting plan, coparents can begin to have business meetings to discuss plans for child caretaking and for assigning responsibilities to each of you. These meetings can be pleasant if both parents attend them with the spirit of putting the children first and of dealing with grief productively. It is at these business meetings that you can talk about what is best for your child and write down arrangements that will work. Coparents who have successful business meetings begin to develop enthusiasm for the future by getting together with a purpose on behalf of their children.

How the business approach helps grief

Emotional control is easier in business than in our personal lives because at work we are not dealing with our crucial human needs. The business approach to coparenting gives mothers and fathers a neutral framework for moving on with the task of setting up life in two homes. When you and your child's other parent can use meetings to settle issues and negotiate plans, you speed up your divorce recovery. Making progress in the coparenting relationship actually gives you both something back – a new kind of connection. Loss and grief are even neutralized when you feel the benefits of this valuable process.

Learning to succeed

A natural but negative response to the idea of becoming parenting business partners can be: "There's no way we can get along! If we could talk to each other so easily, we'd still be together!"

Yet the quality of the coparenting relationship is critical to the foundation of your child's changing family. This means that for the sake of the ones you love, you are going to have to try, even if the beginning is a struggle. Simple rules of procedure will help, especially if both of you use them.

- Make appointments to talk to each other. Impulsive, spur of the moment conversations can set off anger and feelings of grief.

- Be prepared to communicate with your coparent. Bring lists of your concerns and decide ahead of time that you are going to work things out.

- Begin by talking about easy issues, where there already is agreement between you. Harder issues will be easier to address after you have established success.

- Be prepared to adjourn the meeting if things become too emotional, and be prepared to meet again at another time. Learning to coparent well could be described as an art, and like other forms of art, it takes practice.

The primary focus of this parenting guide is to outline strategies for coparents to work with stepparents after they remarry. At the crux of this approach is learning to look at the growing parental network in a way that keeps central your child's needs.

Learn to look at the growing parental network in a way that keeps central your child's needs.

A separated parent who rushes into a new relationship without first forming a decent working relationship with the biological coparent runs into many problems. Former spouses must learn to cooperate with each other before they can expect success with other adults in the picture. This means that spending the time and energy it takes to achieve a positive understanding with your child's other parent will pay off greatly for your family. Once you learn to have meetings to discuss the business of parenting, you will always be able to meet with each other, and whenever serious problems develop with home-to-home parenting you will naturally get together to talk.

The concept of family manners

Acknowledging the importance of the coparenting relationship is one great stride in moving on, but sometimes business meetings fail, and sometimes the conflict is just too high to try. Grief, loss, loneliness, and fear can work to prevent or undo progress. One parent, or both, may be unable to muster up the composure required for the meeting to be productive. In these cases, simple good manners can make a big difference.

While each of the five stages of grief has a hand in the divorce recovery progress, the stage of anger is by far the most troublesome. Anger leads to projection outward in the form of blame, sarcasm, moralizing, or to internalization in the form of self-blame. As a result of these dynamics, acting-out by one or both parents often makes communication impossible. Just when grieving partners need compassion and understanding the most, they become unable to get it from, or give it to, each other.

Conversations similar to the following are the result:

Parent 1: *This situation is all your fault. You created it, now live with it.*

Parent 2: *You have no idea what I am going through. You are the one who has caused all this pain, and you know it.*

These grieving coparents are angry, flinging emotions at each other, and they are certain to fail in moving forward with their coparenting. Worse, they are hurting each other with their words, which will make healing from the loss of the marriage even harder. Neither of them is being careful with what they say, and both are contributing to the conflict.

Acting out with rude and accusatory language is the single most harmful behavior for parents and their children – even in conversations where children are not present. Experts who study verbal abuse have long pointed out the emotional toll it takes on whoever is targeted with the anger and on other members of the family as well. While venting may provide short term relief for the speaker, the long term damage it causes will hurt the entire family.

Use Please and Thank-you, Please

Overcoming angry impulses long enough to use the good manners we learned as children leads to better, more effective dialogue and decision-making after separation. The simple habits of asking nicely for things we want and of thanking others for what they give us are invaluable tools for developing the coparent relationship. Even more important, grief is replaced with a feeling of well-being every time a verbal exchange with a former partner is polite. Coparents who put order back into their lives by turning to productive ways of treating each other are on the road to healing.

> Parent 1: Would you please meet with me to talk about the children?
>
> Parent 2: Yes, and thank you for asking me.

Compared to first conversation in the preceding section, this exchange is far more promising, and far more respectful of the needs of the children.

Acting out with rude and accusatory language is the single most harmful behavior for parents and their children.

The simple habits of asking nicely for things we want and of thanking others for what they give us are invaluable tools for developing the coparent relationship.

Your Personal Commitments

In some families cooperative parenting is difficult or even impossible because one coparent refuses the concept, or is unable to keep the needs of the child first. Even in these instances, though, coparents should make personal, if not joint, oaths to carry out their roles with maturity and the utmost sense of responsibility.

What kinds of personal commitments should coparents make? Consider signing the following document after you have read through the items while thinking about giving your children the loving justice they deserve.

My Personal Commitments

I will always treat my coparent respectfully and courteously. I will make my best effort to promote a positive relationship between my child and the other parent, as well as members of the other household and extended family. I will not say things that could be interpreted as disparaging of the other parent or anyone else loved by my children.

When I have a concern that importantly affects my child, I will make efforts to communicate with my coparent about the concern. I will state the issue clearly, and in a way which will promote communication. I will address one issue at a time, focus on the future, and not make demands.

When I need something from my coparent, I will ask for it in a courteous way. When my coparent has a concern, I will listen and try to help. I will do everything I can to keep conflict between us low. I will keep in mind the benefits of cooperative coparenting, even when it is difficult. I understand that harmonious coparenting is my ultimate goal.

When my child raises issues with my coparent, or with the other home, I will communicate these to my coparent and try to resolve problems peacefully. I will not let the children "split" us further apart. When the children complain, I will take care not to respond as though the child's view is accurate until I have learned the facts and listened to my coparent's perspective.

I will keep our children out of the middle. I will not discuss conflictual issues when they are nearby, and I will not ask them to relay adult messages to the other parent for me. I will not ask my children inappropriate questions about my coparent's personal life. I will not ask them to keep secrets, and I will not burden them with financial or legal matters.

Most importantly, I will strive to celebrate the important moments of my child's life by including my coparent in the celebrations. I will strive for cooperative parenting on these important occasions, which will include ceremonies, graduations, and, someday, the weddings of our children. I will strive to remember that, to our children, both parents are forever.

My Name	**Today's Date**

Helping Children Cope

Children go through the same stages of grief as their parents after divorce, but their reactions take different forms. Since they are vulnerable and helpless, young children often blame themselves for the breakup and feel sad, lonely, guilty, or angry. Older children may act out their grief by developing loyalty conflicts and by siding with one parent or the other. Almost all children would have preferred that their parents stay together and for years harbor a wish for reconciliation.

Parents provide the most comfort to their children when they communicate with them effectively. Learning to talk to boys and girls openly without blaming the other parent is important, and the value of learning to listen well cannot be overstated. Active or *reflective listening* means responding to your children's comments in a way that lets them know you understand and care about how they feel. Then, with reassuring statements about the future, you can give your child relief from anxiety and other negative emotions.

Study this example of reflective listening to see how you can help your child:

> Child: *I hate going over to Mom's house.*
> You: *It sounds like you are upset.*
> Child: *I am! This two-house stuff makes me mad! Why don't you and Mom get back together?*
> You: *I know you don't like going back and forth. But your mom and I can't live together any longer because we weren't happy together. Things will get better before long.*
> Child: *I hope you're right.*

Almost all children would have preferred that their parents stay together and for years harbor a wish for reconciliation.

A child who is still upset may need more help. When you continue to reflect feelings back and respond with reassurance, you give your child hope.

You: *I guess the divorce makes you angry.*
Child: *I hate it.*
You: *I think I understand how you feel.*
Child: *How do you know things will get better? I'm scared things will always be terrible, and we won't be a family.*
You: *Are you feeling afraid of losing your family?*
Child: *Yes. It's weird being at Mom's house without you. I wonder if you're still there for me.*
You: *I see. You know, children with two homes still have just one family. And I will always be here for you. Call me from Mom's whenever you like it! Let's talk about this again, the next time you get back from Mom's house.*
Child: *OK. Thanks for listening, Dad.*

Parents are most effective after divorce when they work hard to understand the feelings and experiences of their children. Boys and girls who sense that they are understood by their parents develop into strong, adaptable youngsters who are optimistic about life and the future.

Boys and girls who sense that they are understood by their parents develop into strong, adaptable youngsters who are optimistic about life and the future.

Life as a Single Person, Not as a Single Parent

Putting a family together sets off wonderful feelings of accomplishment, but taking one apart can be devastating. Divorce and separation create feelings of loneliness in almost everyone going through the process. Especially for a parent who did not even want the split, becoming single with all the responsibilities of parenting can feel overwhelming.

Since marriage is a union between the adult partners, technically divorce affects only the parents, but few mothers and fathers see it that way. How can former partners who are grieving for their children deal with the prospect of setting up two homes for their boys and girls? Again, reframing involves looking at a situation in a way that objectively describes the facts, and in a way that is less emotional. Keep in mind that children will maintain relationships with both mothers and fathers after divorce, and that, as parents, you will transform your personal union into a coparenting relationship. This way you will be taking care of your child side-by-side as the years go by, and you will not be parenting alone.

Even with a good coparenting partnership, becoming a single person after living with a spouse presents a tremendous challenge. Separated adults must learn to do things alone that they used to do together – socially, financially, and practically, in everyday life. Feelings of helplessness and isolation spur many grieving fathers and mothers into finding new partners, or getting into new relationships too quickly. In an effort to deal with horrendous personal loss they bring new adults into their lives for the purpose of personal support. Far too often, though, neither the children nor the parents are really ready to handle this change.

Divorce counselors routinely advise separating parents to "wait" before recoupling, but many lonely former spouses have trouble heeding this advice. To focus on strengthening your

Feelings of helplessness and isolation spur many grieving fathers and mothers into finding new partners, or getting into new relationships too quickly.

coparenting relationship in the early months or years after separation, tell yourself that, although you are single person-ally, you are not a single parent. Far from it; if you do it well, your coparent will always be there as your first resource in help-ing you care for your child. Whether you remarry now, later, or never at all, your child's other parent will be in your life. Many recoupled men and women find this fact distasteful, but part of your job as a parent is to work at accepting reality.

Rebuilding a life of your own

Separated partners who move right on to another relationship get support and emotional help from the new partner they have found. While repartnering so soon may not be best for the children, many grieving spouses couple-up as a coping defense. Even when divorced mothers and fathers claim to have found a more suitable lover after leaving a spouse who "never" was right, most are in denial about the depth of the loss they are feeling. Having a replacement partner seems to make dealing with the loss easier.

It is my belief that parents who stay single longer and, at least for a while, refrain from replacing the intimate partner do a service to their children and their divorced family. Fathers and mothers who wait are more able to put the needs of the child before their own, and can concentrate on healing. Although life may be more painful now, the longer term outlook is better. Taking time to work through the difficult emotions and develop a new sense of yourself will pay off.

One important step in rebuilding your personal life after divorce involves allowing yourself to grieve. While everyone experiences mourning differently, everyone must go through the stages in order to heal and go on with life. This means

Fathers and mothers who wait are more able to put the needs of the child before their own, and can concentrate on healing.

A business relationship exists solely for the sake of the children, and a healthy coparent bond helps cut your sense of loss.

recognizing every day that denial, anger or depression may flare up and interfere with how you cope for as long as it takes to reach acceptance.

Nothing you can do will prevent the process of grief from taking its course, but many things you can do will help. First, recognize your anger and how it affects you as well as your children. Take steps to learn to manage your negative emotions, and recognize that blame is a stumbling block. Next, allow yourself to feel sad, and when you begin to feel better, say so to yourself. The value of positive self-talk is never so important as in difficult situations, and self-statements such as "I know I'll feel better soon" are effective in the healing process.

Another way to help yourself begin to rebuild your life is to focus on the value of friendship. Never before have friends been such a powerful source of support, and letting these relationships flourish now is key. Intentionally counter the tendency to withdraw, and make yourself spend time with your friends. Your self-reliance and independence might be wonderful qualities, but interacting with supportive friends and relatives will give you confidence and courage to keep going.

Perhaps the most important element in rebuilding a sense of personal self after separation is in the evolving coparent relationship itself. This new kind of connection is different from the old relationship because it is not personal or intimate. A business relationship exists solely for the sake of the children, and a healthy coparent bond helps cut your sense of loss. It also helps you develop individual self-awareness while you both work at coparenting. Mothers and fathers who focus on the children while giving themselves time to heal find solace, peace, and a sense of control in the future.

Preparing to integrate new adults into the life of your child
As time goes by after divorce, and as the coparenting relationship becomes solidified, healing mothers and fathers become
sufficiently confident that they will always put the needs of
their children first. Good coparents internalize new habits of
talking to each other about the needs of their boys and girls,
and of yielding to each other in compromise. By doing this
carefully and thoughtfully, you are preparing yourself to bring
a new partner into your child's world when the time is right.

The basic premise of this guide is that your child's family
will always have the biological parents at the head. Your own
personal world may grow to include a lover who is outside
your child's love-reality, and you will want this person to enter
your child's world. The role he or she will play, however, will
be different from that of a natural parent. All coparents who
want the best for their children carry this understanding with
them as they go forward in their lives.

Chapter 2

REMARRIAGE: A SECOND CHANCE

Great Expectations

Three out of four men and women who divorce remarry, and most of these have children. Two basic motivations explain this high rate of recoupling. First, as a consequence of guilt and grief, divorced parents want to fix things for their children by making the family whole again. The second reason is simple and possibly more compelling — divorce represents failure, and people want to succeed.

Both reasons for remarriage are legitimate. Our culture promotes the value of having a strong family, and the preferred stereotype of a two-parent home is still with us. We therapists work with single parents to help them view themselves as unique family units, but the stigma of remaining "single" still leads us to images of a "broken" family.

A divorced parent's remarriage symbolizes many things, including a second chance at happiness. Coparents who remarry demonstrate to the world their determination, and they send a message to the former spouse that they will be happy again. Whether the second marriage comes early after divorce, or later, the goal is always the same — to find joy and personal satisfaction.

In this chapter I discuss the complexities of stepfamily dynamics and begin to outline reasons why problems develop between the first and second families. A coparent marrying someone who has never been married and has no children will face very different circumstances from one who remarries another divorced person with children. A divorced parent who chooses to stay single while the other parent remarries will have to cope with being outnumbered. In essence, the number of options and potential for knotty interactional situations is almost unimaginable when people with children remarry.

The number of options and potential for knotty interactional situations is almost unimaginable when people with children remarry.

Dreams That Don't Come True

Once the decision is made to remarry, the thought of the pending wedding can cause exuberance in a coparent still recovering from divorce. Visions of restored family unity and pleasurable times ahead often lead to feelings of ecstasy, even for those realistic enough to know that creating a stepfamily can be difficult. Here the dynamic of denial takes over as plans are made for the ceremony, honeymoon, and a home together. Even when there are warning signs of trouble to come, they are often overlooked because of the new couple's immense resolve for success.

In spite of the enthusiasm partners share at the time of the second marriage, we have found that the first two years are the most difficult time for a stepfamily. After the initial celebration, problems begin to surface which were not anticipated, and stress begins to rise. Along with handling the typical pressures of child rearing, both partners must cope with adults in the other household and try to juggle everyone's needs. The weight of trying to solidify the new commitment amidst all the issues with parenting can be substantial. Statistics show that stepfamilies are at a greatest risk for failure during the first two years after marriage.

Consider the following script:

Still unmarried at 33, a woman is delighted that she has fallen in love with a wonderful man. He is the father of two appealing children. She accepts his proposal to marry and to help him with the parenting. Several months after a wonderful start and early warm feelings all around, the children begin to pull away from their stepmother, envious of the attention their father pays his wife. Next, conflict develops for the parent and stepparent as the father pulls away to align himself with the children. The stepmother now feels abandoned and questions her decision to marry.

This woman entered marriage knowing she would have to work hard at her new role, but not anticipating the feelings she would experience when other changes took place. As the children's troublesome reactions began to emerge, and reality set in, her dreams of lasting happiness became threatened.

Many other versions of shattered dream scenarios occur. Men who marry overworked women with children are often disappointed when their efforts to be involved are rejected by a child, the children's father, or even the new spouse herself. Women who marry exclusively for love in a second relationship can become disgruntled by the disappearance of romance within a very short time. Women and men who both have children often become disillusioned by problems that multiply when three or four different homes are involved.

Despite the problems faced by divorced and remarried parents, and despite our culture's depiction of these problems in books, television and movies, thousands of stepfamilies are formed every day. The dreams and primal drives of men, women and children to live together in groups are just too strong to be overcome by the prospect of difficulties. Parents who remarry have no choice but to try to create happy lives in all their children's homes.

Stages and Tasks of the Stepfamily

Experts who study second marriages, notably James H. Bray, have found that several basic stages of development affect almost every stepfamily. Individual differences occur because of unique factors in families, but certain patterns are repeated. Making adjustments and accepting challenges will be easier if you become familiar with these stages, so you can be ready to be flexible when you need to.

The three general stages can be described as:

Stage 1   Initial adjustment

Stage 2   Familiarity after settling in

Stage 3   Transitions in later years

Stage 1. Initial Adjustment

The first two years of stepfamily life are almost always difficult. Everyday demands call for so many changes in old habits that stress and resistance are experienced by spouses, new stepparents, and children who have instantly acquired new parents or siblings. When the divorced coparents have not successfully worked out their business relationship, there will also be conflict between households. All members of the newly formed family may feel a loss of the privacy and separateness enjoyed before the marriage. Even worse, grief usually intrudes once again, reminding parents and children of their losses, and both sadness and anger emerge about the past.

Stepfamilies that successfully get through the difficult first phase of remarriage are able to accomplish several important things:

1. **Husband and wife are able to focus on the new marital unit and develop a strong marital bond while at the same time putting the needs of the children above their own.** They can resist forces trying to split them, which come from the children or from adults in the other home. Spouses who thrive as a couple after the first stage of remarriage acquire a vocabulary that reflects their sense of "we" and "us," and this strong connection outlasts conflict and confusion.

2. **Stepparents are able to develop appropriate roles for themselves in relation to the new spouses' children.** The bonding process is started, and both coparent and stepparent can distinguish their marriage from their roles as parents. Respect is maintained for the primacy of the relationship between two original parents and biological children, and

When the divorced coparents have not successfully worked out their business relationship, there will also be conflict between households.

stepparents willingly step back when necessary. Ideas for learning to do this appear further on in this chapter and in later chapters of this guide.

3. **The child's parents and stepparents learn to work out problems with coparenting across two homes.** Second families who thrive after the first two years have found ways of negotiating with adults in the other household that are flexible, reasonable, and successful, at least for part of the time. When remarried adults cling to rigid ideas, they are much less likely to find peace in the extended family; the best outlook goes to those who are able to yield to each other.

One message of this book is that parents have the power to make their children's lives happy after divorce and remarriage. The overall quality of family life will hinge upon the motivation and efforts of all parent figures to strive for balance, flexibility, and tolerance in how they work together.

Stage 2. Familiarity After Settling In

Life after the first two years is often the best in stepfamilies, when habits and new ways of living have become familiar. Children who were young at the time of remarriage are somewhat older now, more accustomed to family routines, and have passed the initial obstacles of adjustment. Coparents who remarried when their children were already approaching the preteen years, of course, may still struggle at this point, as adolescents are almost always a challenge. Most noticeable, however, is that after the first two years of stepfamily life, fully committed spouses who have weathered early stressors have learned the value of patience. Parents in stepfamilies that flourish learn to trust that life "goes on," not entirely without conflict, but with acceptable resolution of conflicts as they arise.

Two distinct qualities are found in stepfamilies still thriving after the middle phase of development:

1. **Stepparents have formed satisfying relationships with stepchildren and are proud to be related to them through marriage.** This is not to say that either the child or stepparent must claim to "love" the other, but rather that comfort and respect define the connection. Understandably and almost universally, adults and children alike report being unable to develop the same depth of love for a non-biological relative that they have for members of the original family. Feelings and emotions simply cannot be legislated, and many happy stepchildren talk only of "liking" or "being close" to a stepparent.

2. **Coparents in both homes have largely recovered from grief and have developed positive working relationships.** Remarried mothers and fathers are able to attend the children's school or community activities when the child's other parent or a stepparent is there. Scheduling and parenting problems are ironed out as they arise, and new spouses accept the permanent business partnership of each child's biological father and mother. When things are going well, it is usually midway into stepfamily life that first and second spouses of a parent become able to relate to each other in a deeper, friendlier way. Children whose parents all get along are less likely to have problems as they grow into adolescence, simply because they are happier.

The importance of maintaining a strong marital unit continues throughout all three stages of stepfamily life. When conflict arises, partners should turn to each other for help, rather than turning away. It may help to be reminded that after the children are grown, all marriages are solely for the spouses, and those with the strongest personal unions will be the happiest.

Feelings and emotions simply cannot be legislated, and many happy stepchildren talk only of "liking" or "being close" to a stepparent.

Even after doing well for several years, adolescents may shift loyalties, align themselves with a parent in the other home, or rebel against expectations in both homes.

Stage 3. Transitions in Later Years

Later in the lives of stepfamilies, conflict can creep back in. Older children and teens naturally pull away in the process of individuation, which prepares them for leaving home. Even after doing well for several years, adolescents may shift loyalties, align themselves with a parent in the other home, or rebel against expectations in both homes. In this stage, change is inevitable because children will, in fact, soon move out or go to college. Issues surrounding coparenting and stepparenting are critically important as boys and girls become young adults.

Stepfamilies that successfully make it through the final phase of development have one distinct quality: coparents and stepparents in both homes are able to help children prepare to leave home and make plans for emancipation. By doing this, original and remarried spouses keep the child's needs first throughout the teenage years and are paving the way for everyone's happiness later in life.

When families of remarriage continue to struggle rather than flourish, it is often because the parents are too eager to "finish" the task of childrearing. Turning the focus to their own needs and wants while the children are in their teens, some mothers and fathers get tired of parenting and let go of their children too soon. Assuming an adolescent will be able to figure out the future alone, single or remarried parents can fail to maintain the level of attention their older children need in order to move into young adulthood. Later, these young adults have trouble reaching maturity because they did not receive the attentive parenting they needed to become self-sufficient.

The basic idea of keeping your children's needs as your first priority means maintaining this focus until they become autonomous. Your family life will go on for years after the children leave home, and you will want to make these years good. Even after this third major stage of stepfamily growth, there will be other stages to come. How well your family progresses as your children reach adulthood will depend on three things: how well you are able to adapt, your level of marital commitment, and the quality of the coparent and stepparent relationships across homes.

All About Boundaries

The concept of the boundary is especially important for parents in second marriages to understand. A boundary is simply an imagined line drawn around a family member, or around the entire household, to structure personal space. Boundaries may be physical, as when a parent or child needs room to be alone, or emotional, as when privacy about sharing thoughts and feelings is respected.

Even in original families where parents and children are biologically related, family members need personal space. Fathers and mothers have privacy in their bedrooms, and children are given furniture, closets, and rooms of their own whenever possible. Through "ownership" of some section of the family home each child and adult experiences control and safety — physically and emotionally. It is in this zone of comfort that family members become secure and confident.

When parents of first families separate, the boundaries that developed in their household change. They set up indepen-

Many problems in early stepfamily life are related to boundary issues.

dent homes, and the children transition in and out of both of them. A transparent but definite line is drawn between the homes, both of which belong to the children, but not the parents. Coparents are asked to respect this boundary between residences, and not to enter each other's home without invitation. When divorced parents transform their personal relationship into a business relationship without intimacy, they put new limits on how they relate. Children also learn the reality of the two-home concept and begin to accept the boundaries of their future.

If you are a separated parent thinking about bringing a new adult into your child's life, it will help to remember the idea of the boundary. Children and adults who do not share genes often need even more personal and emotional space than they had in the original family. Men and women accustomed to living alone may not want to be in the company of children for long periods of time. Older children and teens, especially, will not instantly feel affection for any new parenting figure and will often pull away to create the distance they need. Many problems in early stepfamily life are related to boundary issues.

Two kinds of fear explain problems with boundaries in second families:

- *Fear of loss – of losing a sense of identity, or a bond to the original family*
- *Fear of rejection – of not being liked, respected, or accepted*

The following examples illustrate how lack of important boundaries can cause problems in a second family:

Example 1

A seven-year-old girl is accustomed to running into her dad's bedroom on Saturday and Sunday mornings, giving him a kiss and talking about the upcoming day. After remarriage the dad's new wife objects to this habit, expressing her feeling that the child intrudes on their privacy. Afraid to disappoint his daughter, the father refuses to tell her she must wait until breakfast to talk, and the wife becomes upset with her new spouse.

Failing to set a reasonable limit on the child's behavior will cause stress in the new relationship, but failing to deal with the child's fear of losing a bond with her father will also be troublesome. As you will see throughout this book, *balance* is often the key. This man can resolve the dilemma by setting a boundary with his daughter for the sake of his wife's feelings, and by finding other ways to connect with his child:

> "I am going to ask that you stay in your own bedroom until 8 o'clock on Saturday and Sunday mornings. Then, after I come to your room to get you, the two of us will make breakfast together, okay?"

The second example illustrates the importance of personal time and space to a child:

Example 2

A fourteen-year-old boy whose mother has just remarried is spending a great deal of time in his room. Though they know this could be natural for a teenager, both the mother and new stepfather are offended by the child's habit of withdrawing from them. Together they insist that he join them at the dining room table for meals, in the family room to watch movies, and in the *kitchen to do his homework. The boy becomes furious with his mother, and calls his father in the other home to complain.*

Here the child is really objecting to being forced to adjust to changes too quickly. His room is his safe haven from the anxiety he feels, perhaps around sharing his mother with another male, or to his fear of relating to his stepfather. If the mother and stepfather feel meals should be time spent together, allowing the boy to do homework alone will honor his need for privacy.

Since the first two years of stepfamily life are the most difficult, parents in new second marriages have a better chance of success when they pay close attention to the matter of boundaries, both within and between the two homes. In later chapters of this book we will see how coparents and stepparents are most effective when they have mastered reasonable ways of guiding and disciplining the children. Whenever problems created by boundary issues appear, resolving them with balance is advised.

Building the Marital Bond

The first predictor of stepfamily success is the quality of the marital bond, and working on the marriage itself is fundamental. Even before the wedding, adults who want to be married forever should make a special kind of commitment to each other. This promise means intending to ride out waves of trouble and conflict that are inevitable in a second marriage with children. At the core is an understanding that, no matter what, *we will still be together* when the children are grown.

The best strategy for actively building the marital bond involves following a few basic principles:

1. **Make time for working together, and time for playing together.** For many people, life in a second marriage comes with instant children. In first marriages there is usually time for the couple to bond through basic activities of life before a child is born, but after remarriage spouses must intentionally take this time. Scheduled activities, like doing yard work together or going out on "dates," are bonding opportunities that you will need to create.

2. **Get to know your spouse as well as you can.** Again, the distractions of parenting can interfere if you let them, and you may gradually abandon the important tasks of learning more about each other and nurturing your mutual love. Recoupled men and women come with complex pasts and histories, and understanding the needs, wants, and wishes of your spouse should not be postponed. Make it your priority now, as well as in the future.

3. **Turn to your partner for help.** Perhaps the single most damaging dynamic in any marriage occurs when spouses fail to communicate their feelings, suffer in isolation because they don't feel supported, and then turn to outsiders for understanding. Conflict is inevitable in any relationship, but after divorce and remarriage, the need to resolve it between you is primary. Remember that every time you successfully work through a problem, you deepen your personal bond.

4. **Be willing to change for your spouse.** The importance of yielding in a second marriage is greater than in a first because there are more areas for conflict and because the consequences

can be dire. As a parent worried about the happiness of your child, you may be prone to overlooking your spouse's needs, or as a spouse without biological children, you may not understand your partner's dilemma. Tell yourself that by changing or making sacrifices you won't be giving up too much. Your partner will appreciate your efforts and will be more willing to change for you.

$5.$ **Remember the power of "us."** In every second family with children, the business of everyday life includes the boys and girls of one or both new spouses. As weeks and months go by, however, it will be the amount of couple-identity the two of you manage to maintain that will determine your marital satisfaction. During the years while the children are growing up, it will never really be "just us" because the children will need so much of your time. In later years, though, your sense of well-being and happiness will depend on the sense of "us" that you have nurtured, and you can work on this from the beginning.

Shaping the quality of your second partnership is entirely within your power if you follow these basic guidelines. Divorced coparents should still keep the needs of their children first, but remember that focusing on the new marital bond will always be critical for you and your children as well. Chapters that follow suggest ways to balance the needs of children with the needs of adults in the marital relationship.

Bonding With A Stepchild

Children in first families naturally bond to their parents because of day-to-day contact in caretaking from the very moment of birth. In stepfamilies the bonding process is more difficult, but it is just as important. Whether or not a legal second marriage takes place, intimate partners who enter the lives of separated parents greatly impact the children. However, men and women take on roles of stepparent or stepparent "figure" with varying amounts of determination and intent. As a result, confusion often develops with regard to when, how, and whether this bonding should take place.

Before you begin to bond

Keeping the needs of the children first, stepparent figures should first decide with their partner about whether a stronger attachment would be good for the child or whether it presents an emotional risk. Experts generally agree that until a new adult relationship involves a substantial degree of commitment, a coparent's "significant other" should at best become an *acquaintance* of the child or children. Acquaintances are not close or personal relationships, and child and adult do not usually spend time together, except briefly.

Only after the divorced parent is ready to settle into a committed arrangement with the new partner should the process of bonding begin. This guideline recognizes the substantial loss the child has already experienced, and respects the child's vulnerability to further loss. Children who grow fond of their parents' new partners only to lose them again when relationships fail will suffer significant harm.

Coparents looking for a general guideline about when it is safe to bring new adults into the lives of their children can follow the **"six-month rule."** This means that six months after separation, and six months after you have formed a decent coparenting relationship, a child may be ready for an acquaintance

Only after the divorced parent is ready to settle into a committed arrangement with the new partner should the process of bonding begin.

to be introduced. Then, after six more months of your children being acquainted but uninvolved with your new partner, simultaneously letting time go by for your child to adjust to the new two-home reality, he or she may be ready to get to know your partner better. By allowing six months of time to pass at each stage in the bonding process, you will create a climate of acceptance for your daughter or son.

Ages and stages in development

In general there is an inverse relationship between a child's age and his or her ability to bond easily with a stepparent, even one who is very loving. Younger children easily form multiple attachments to interested adults and willingly let stepparents into their emotional world. Older children, though, are more wary, and because they have deeper bonds with their original parents, they are less likely to bond in ways that feel natural. Teenagers, especially, may never feel close to stepparents, at least partly because they are pulling away from even the natural parents as they become more independent.

The paradox of the bonding dilemma is that although a young child may bond most easily with a new stepparent, the coparent in the other home is also most likely to object to this bonding when the child is young. The majority of parents divorce when their children are under ten years of age, and feelings of ownership still affect the process of separation. Unable to "let go" of the child just yet, and not yet able to accept the eventuality of a stepparent's bond, a divorced parent still grieving will often resist a new person becoming important to a beloved child. New stepparents who understand and respect this dynamic will not press for closeness too soon.

By allowing six months of time to pass at each stage in the bonding process, you will create a climate of acceptance for your daughter or son.

Steps in the bonding process

Stepparents and significant committed adults in the restructured family can and should intentionally work on developing healthy relationships with a partner's child. The child's parent may need to talk to his or her coparent to develop a joint philosophy about accepting a new parenting partner. Stepmothers and stepfathers do not replace natural parents, but children do gain additional caretakers when their parents remarry or recouple in permanence. Loving parents faced with feelings of jealousy because a new adult is involved with the child should practice thinking about the child's family as including all members of both households. Try to think of your child's stepparent as an additional care provider rather than as someone taking over your role.

Bonding with a stepchild can be looked at as a process taking place gradually over time, and we can identify five general stages:

Stage 1. Becoming acquainted.

At first the adult and child spend time together in the presence of the natural parent, doing non-intimate activities such as going to movies or eating out. Talking in the presence of the biological parent about the child's interests, for instance, lets the stepparent get to know the child, who feels safe in the company of his or her parent.

Stage 2. "Joining" with the child.

Next, without the biological parent the child and adult do activities together that the child already enjoys, such as attending sporting events or going shopping. Spending time doing familiar activities makes being together without the natural

Try to think of your child's stepparent as an additional care provider rather than as someone taking over your role.

parent start to feel right. Having fun doing something the child enjoys is a *must* for building a positive bond.

Stage 3. Creating caring between you.

This stage might be described as friendship between stepparent and stepchild. Trust has begun to develop, and each looks forward to seeing the other. The child begins to care about the new stepparent's feelings and opinions, and both stepparent and child become more concerned about each other's well-being.

Stage 4. Deepening the new relationship.

After a solid base of mutual caring and respect has been built, a stepparent who begins to feel responsible for guiding the child can move into a more parental role. A child who has grown to understand and trust a stepparent will accept his or her influence without feeling resentful. Parents and children in happy stepfamilies often report having reached this stage in the bonding process.

Stage 5. Love between stepchild and stepparent.

The most gratifying relationships in families are those in which there is mutual love. Because there are so many complexities in stepfamilies, though, and because feelings are very personal, this deepest stage of bonding often never occurs. This means it is best to have a goal of creating mutual trust and caring because love is not a necessary ingredient for happiness between stepparent and stepchild.

The importance of the stepparent relationship should be recognized as a wonderful resource for children, but it is too often undervalued. After suffering the losses inevitable with divorce, children and new parents alike can get immense satisfaction from these new connections, which come ready-made to work on. In fact, children experience an additional loss when a stepparent fails to move in closer and opts not to bond in any way.

A more damaging dynamic than under-bonding with a stepchild develops when a stepparent feels entitled and take on the role of strict disciplinarian. The problem is that unpleasant or punitive interactions between a child and adult, especially in the early stages of a relationship, will block your efforts to become close and will undermine the bonding process. Only biological parents or grandparents with existing bonds should administer reprimands or discipline.

Because of the importance of stepparent-stepchild attachment, coparents themselves should always discipline their sons and daughters, especially when it comes to punishment. This topic is a crucial one, and in Chapter 7 I include a detailed plan for sorting through the input about discipline from the stepparent while leaving the biological parent in charge.

The Power of Language and Labels

As humans we are sophisticated beings, capable of thinking very quickly. Putting thoughts into words, however, slows down our thinking process and brings emotion into how we communicate. The words and phrases we speak to others reflect our underlying attitudes about them and greatly influence how we are perceived.

In the world of divorce and remarriage, many of our terms are unpleasant. Spouses recently separated often avoid the word "divorce" because of the negative meaning it suggests, and chil-

The words and phrases we speak to others reflect our underlying attitudes about them and greatly influence how we are perceived.

dren are often slow to accept it as well. The word "stepfamily" carries mixed and controversial meaning, and not all adults who remarry like the label. Describing a family as "blended" can erase the sense of individuality needed by separate family members, and adjectives such as "mixed" or "reconstituted" are unpalatable. Perhaps the most destructive use of a label happens when stepmothers are called "wicked," in the vein of an ugly fairytale.

This problem of negativity in language and labels adds to the experience of grief. In contrast to negative words describing divorce, our terms for original families are all positive, and create pleasant images of harmony. The words *mother, father, child,* and *home* seem lovely when compared to those that reflect the loss-history of second families. Perhaps the worst of these terms, *broken home,* implies pain, grief, and suffering. The words *stepmother, stepfather,* and *stepchild* actually evolved from the loss caused by death.

As the structure of family continues to change in our culture, better, more neutral terms to describe its character and components will develop. In Chapter 3 I introduce the term *cross-parent* to refer to same-sex parents in separate homes who both take part in rearing children. Other words or phrases are sure to appear as they are needed to ease relations between family members. Currently, for example, there is no way to describe relationships between former stepsiblings who once were related when their parents were in a second marriage, but who now have gone through divorce again. The concept of the ex-stepbrother or sister seems so difficult to acknowledge that cultural denial has perpetuated our lack of language to even describe it.

The Use of Language in Relationships

When people are looking for love they are careful about how they talk to each other. Wanting to please a potential partner and be certain he or she sees the best in us, we are gracious, polite, and mannerly in early dating conversations. It is simply human nature that, to "win friends and influence people," any individual wanting to build a positive relationship will use words that are supportive and encouraging.

In later stages of a relationship, such as after months or years of a marriage, partners become more casual in their styles of talking to each other. Deeper personal needs that have been put aside for the sake of winning a spouse reappear, and feelings about each other change. Communications may begin to reflect anger and frustration about each partner's wants or needs, and spouses can try to control each other with words. Some become subtly manipulative, others more abusive, and dynamics that lead to separation begin to develop.

By the time a relationship is over, many divorcing spouses are in such conflict they are unable to move forward and heal. Using a language of negativity to process their grief, many men and women perpetuate blame and resort to hurtful labeling to get by. After all, dealing with the loss of a "good for nothing" husband or a "nagging, deceitful" wife is easier than coping with the loss of a "wonderful" woman or man.

The language chosen to be used by spouses after remarriage is more important than ever before. Stepfamilies come with many problems, unresolved issues, and leftover negative feelings. Angry coparents who communicated poorly to begin with and who continue the tirades or relentless blame after recoupling bring impending disaster to their new homes. The worst damage will be to the children, who will be hurt by witnessing verbal abuse between their parents.

Separation always causes inevitable feelings of loss, grief, and failure. But ongoing negative talk by parents across two households, even when disguised as the "truth," stresses children and stepchildren trying to cope. The self-esteem of boys and girls is dramatically lowered when they know their parents disapprove of each other, and when new partners of their former spouses are not accepted. When parents continue the verbal battle after divorce and remarriage, they weaken their children's future abilities to handle the world successfully.

Verbal manners seem to have gone out of style, but for the sake of children they love, mothers, fathers and stepparents should resurrect the niceties of language.

Your Stepfamily's New Identity

Parents in stepfamilies are generally older than those in original marriages. In addition, every second marriage also comes after a first – each partner has had more life experience and brings more history to the family. Children from first marriages bring their individual personalities to the family and also bring their feelings about their parents' divorce. Each new stepfamily will eventually become a unique combination of these elements, plus much more.

Two important factors contribute to the development of every family's identity. The first is how each parent's past has affected

Ongoing negative talk by parents across two households, even when disguised as the "truth," stresses children and stepchildren trying to cope.

them in childhood, in early adulthood, and in prior relationships. Sometimes referred to as "baggage," your past experiences, good or bad, come with you into your stepfamily.

Consider the following scenarios:

A spouse who grew up in poverty and was then financially strapped in a first marriage is determined to do better in the second marriage. This spouse is worried about the new family's budget, and may push for a frugal lifestyle while trying to save money by working long hours.

A spouse who divorced because the first mate was lethargic and inactive is driven to be on the go in the new marriage. This spouse strives for a hectic, overactive and carefree new lifestyle, to "make up for lost time" in the past.

Because children are innocent victims of divorce, their needs should be the first priority of parents in second marriages. Parents and stepparents committed to their girls' and boys' well-being are alert to the dangers of shaping the new family's character only according to their own needs. The examples above illustrate that overemphasis on saving money, having fun, or other personal priorities, while important to the adults, may not be best for the children.

The second important factor that helps mold the new family is how personal need for space plays out among parents and children. Problems created by boundary issues can account for many of a stepfamily's conflicts during the first two years while the family personality is being formed. Children accustomed to having their own bedrooms who are asked to share with stepsiblings resist, usually feeling "forced" to give up their privacy. Coparents trying to talk to each other by phone feel "intruded upon" by new spouses who hover over them. Spouses who marry coparents with strong healthy bonds to their children can feel "lost" in the second family, like visitors outside the boundaries of the real family unit.

Developing a unique family style takes time and flexibility. Each family member must first get enough of what he or she needs to feel satisfied. Demands for togetherness will not work when parents or children have needs for space which are not being met. Strict rules that force blending will fail, but a structure for working out ways to live with and around each other will help. Adaptability and equilibrium should be the goals of the parents in creating a family style, especially when the children have two family personalities to live with because both of the parents have remarried.

The stepfamily household meeting

The best way for a stepfamily to work on finding a unique identity is to have regular family meetings. These structured get-togethers with the children serve the important function of giving every family member a chance to express feelings and needs in a forum of acceptance. An even greater benefit is the sense of belonging the meetings impart to everyone in the family. The act of sitting down as a family unit for the purpose of communication can be invaluable.

The format of the stepfamily meeting is simple. Coparent and stepparent select a time and place and notify the children of the meeting. Begin by sharing compliments about each other or by talking about good things that have happened. Next, the meeting's leader – which is usually a parent – asks for issues to be brought up, and these are discussed one by one. Certain rules of procedure are followed, such as allowing only one family

Demands for togetherness will not work when parents or children have needs for space which are not being met.

member to speak at a time and having someone act as "secretary" to record the topics discussed. Decisions can be made about how things will be handled in the family, and plans can emerge for lowering conflict between family members.

Study the following example of how one stepfamily grew stronger by having a family meeting:

After several months of a second marriage, a remarried mother and her new husband were having problems with the children. The woman's six-year-old son was making life miserable for the stepfather and for his eight-year-old daughter, who spent time in the home on weekends. The boy called the girl nasty names and stated that he wished she would die. Upset and needing to do something, the parents set up a family meeting.

The meeting began with the mother complimenting her son for picking up his toys earlier that day, and with the father complimenting his daughter's new outfit. Then the mother asked if either child had a complaint to talk about, and her son said he wished his stepsister would stop coming over on weekends. His stepfather asked the boy to talk about his feelings, and the boy began to cry. Soon the child expressed his wish that his original parents would get back together, and his underlying grief about his parents' divorce became obvious. A helpful dialogue followed and the child was able to apologize to his stepsister.

The meeting ended with the mother planning to spend one-on-one time playing cards with her son, and by promising to call the boy's father to talk about their little boy's sadness. The child seemed relieved to have been heard in the family meeting, and all family members said they "felt better." This stepfamily's identity will be characterized by productive communication.

Most outcomes of family meetings are less dramatic than this example, but still result in the development of individual family habits. Holiday celebrations are planned, accomplishments of family members are reviewed, and requests are made for ways to develop important new traditions. A family's identity becomes unique as new habits and ways of doing things emerge, and as children and parents alike begin to look forward to being together. The family meeting itself can become an invaluable ritual, and through its repetition the family develops a past. Creating a positive history by talking, planning, and solving problems together over time gives children, coparents, and stepparents a unique sense of "us" as a family unit.

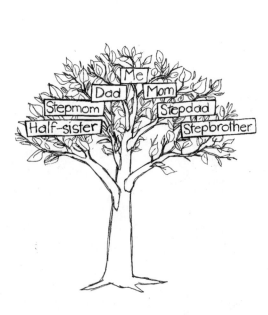

Chapter 3

COPARENTS, STEPPARENTS, & CROSSPARENTS

Structure in the Parenting Network

When a divorced parent remarries and brings a stepparent into the family, this new partner has another important relationship to work through — with the parent in the other home. I call the relationship between a parent and a stepparent of the same sex: *crossparent*. The two of you fill similar, but not equal roles. A stepmother enters a relationship with the family-of-origin mother, and a stepfather assumes one with the family-of-origin father. To varying degrees, stepparents in each restructured household will need to relate to each other as well, whenever both homes have added these new parenting figures.

When both coparents recouple, either through marriage or stable live-in relationships, the number of parent connections in your child's family multiplies. The diagram on the following page illustrates family structure after both coparents remarry. Originally there was only one parental relationship, but now

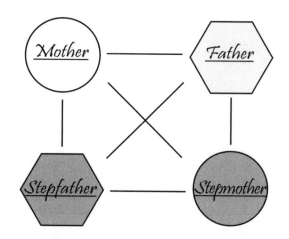

there are six in the network. With this fact in mind, I find it no surprise that complications and disagreements about parenting issues appear.

Roles, Rules, and Confusion

The following kinds of questions frequently asked by new stepparents and coparents reflect the confusion so often experienced:

* Stepmother: *How much should I do for the children? Should I make the school lunches or should their father do it? Where do I fit in?*

* Stepfather: *I've always been the man of the house. Now do I let the children's mother run things? Am I supposed to change?*

* Coparent mother: *Should I coach the children's stepmother*

on what each one of them needs, or let her figure things out on her own?

◆ Coparent father: *Am I supposed to become a friend of the children's new stepfather just because he married my former wife?*

No precise directory exists that defines the roles of stepparents or outlines how crossparents should relate, but there are some general guidelines that you can apply. These are based on the premise that the children's needs should come first to you, and that the child's original parents will always come first to them.

1. A general rule for stepparents is to **take small steps into the active parenting arena while respecting the child's need for consistency in the primary parental relationship.** For example, the stepmother in the first scenario above may start by shopping for tasty lunch items while the father makes the lunches for the children. The stepfather in the second example, accustomed to being in control, might negotiate with his new wife that he will be in charge of building a play area in the yard while she deals with the children about their chores.

2. A general rule for the coparent to follow when a crossparent comes into the picture is to **allow these small steps to be taken and to acknowledge the stepparent's presence.** The coparent mother in the third scenario above might ask the new stepmother if she would like to learn more about the children from her, and in doing this she would strengthen the crossparent relationship. The coparent father in the last example might begin by simply saying "hello" to his crossparent, the stepfather. Over time, the two father figures might become

more acquainted and find out what each of them can do for the children.

Even when stepparents, coparents and crossparents have begun to accept each others' roles, questions and anxiety can gnaw at responsible adults. The myriad of circumstances affecting reconstructed families is endless, and all parent-partners can be at a loss as to how to handle things. In keeping with the principle of putting children first, one general rule to follow is: *create a comfort zone for your child by integrating new partners slowly.*

The Ever-Present Veil of Grief

Remarriage is a step directed at putting an end to the loss caused by divorce. Solid second commitments can accomplish this goal, but only when coparents and new spouses recognize and accept that grief takes years to resolve. To some extent you will always grieve the loss of your first marriage, and your children will grieve the loss too. The pathway to emotional healing can be shortened when the milestone of remarriage has been reached, but it cannot be removed entirely. Divorce will always be in your past, along with your cherished memories — good, bad and sad.

Think about a set of parents who married as very young sweethearts, and who enjoyed several years together before they divorced, moved on, and remarried. Sometime later, after years have gone by and problems have emerged in a second marriage, sadness and a sense of loss reappear. One or the other partner from the original marriage may begin to long for the "good old days" and crave the carefree quality of the couple's original love. Knowing he or she cannot go back, however, can only foster feelings of unspoken grief.

In another situation, a mother and father divorced for several years may have worked out comfortable routines, thinking they have healed from divorce and that they have accepted loss fairly well. Then one former partner remarries, disrupting the sense of balance they have achieved, and unexpected turmoil results. Remembering what they once had together, coparents who had been doing well are now reminded of their loss, and become sad or angry with each other. The parent left out of remarriage usually grieves most heavily, faced with the stark reality of what he or she feels should have been in the first place, which is that the marriage should not have failed.

Grief creeps in over the years at every point the family constellation changes, with the addition or loss of family members. A second or third divorce may cause a mother or father to feel utter failure as a parent. Children who gain new stepsiblings only to lose them later through another divorce face emotional complications. Whenever a new child is born into a stepfamily, joy may come to the remarried parents, but sorrow may come to the divorced outsider coparent, and even to the infant's half-siblings.

To some extent you will always grieve the loss of your first marriage, and your children will grieve the loss too.

Parallel Parenting Across Households

Integrating new stepparents into a family first run by coparents in separate homes is always difficult. Even when spouses of the original marriage believe they have healed from grief and have worked out ways of cooperating with each other, adding new caretakers stresses the parenting system. Angry feelings between divorced coparents can rise, and stricter boundaries may need to be drawn. Especially when parents recouple too soon after divorce, limits may need to be set temporarily to protect the children from conflict.

Parallel parenting is a caretaking style that involves less direct communication than cooperative parenting after divorce. Because it reduces conflict, this method of coparenting is often advisable in early stages of a stepfamily, such as the first two years, if negative emotions have begun to surface. Then, as roles of the parent, stepparent, and crossparent become defined, and as unwritten rules become clearer, all caretakers can increase direct communication with adults in the other home.

Divorced and remarried parents who resort to parallel parenting run their households completely separately, and each respects the other's right to do so. Neither parent is obligated to attend activities or special events for the children, and neither one schedules events on the other parent's time. Very exact time-sharing schedules are kept, and coparents communicate only in writing, advising each other about the children's needs. Conflict is effectively controlled with this technique because there is so little parent interaction.

If the overriding rule of parenting after divorce and remarriage is *putting the child's needs first,* I believe parallel parenting should only be instituted as a temporary measure and not as a permanent style of coparenting. Imagine how your children would feel to have two sets of parents who could never talk about them and who would not make the effort to work together. For all its helpfulness in reducing conflict, parallel parenting builds rigidity into the parenting system and prohibits flexibility, the most important component of success.

Over time, and with the help of tools presented later in this manual, coparents and stepparents should strive to give up parallel parenting as an ongoing working method. Whenever stress rises or serious problems develop across homes, however, this kind of parenting should be considered as a stopgap measure for conflict reduction. Children thrive in an environment of parental cooperation, and they suffer in one of judgement, disapproval, or hostility.

The Continuum of Cooperation

As parents separate and finalize a legal divorce, they are assigned responsibility, or custody, of their children. Both are given designated periods of parenting time, and both are usually given rights to make decisions on behalf of their boys and girls. How well divorced parents make these decisions together determines the quality of the coparental relationship.

Research over the past twenty years has consistently shown that it is not the divorce itself that hurts a child. Rather, it is the level of conflict as opposed to cooperation between parents that causes harm. Children raised in an atmosphere of hostility become poorly adjusted adults, whether their parents divorce or not. The very worst outcome for children occurs when they suffer the loss of divorce and bear the burden of their parents' continuing conflict.

After parents remarry there are three or four parents in the system. There are also more sources of disagreement between all parents concerned about the children. Life is busier when

For all its helpfulness in reducing conflict, parallel parenting builds rigidity into the parenting system and prohibits flexibility, the most important component of success.

more people are involved, and new partners have opinions about how time and activities should be arranged. Frustrated coparents with new spouses sometimes try to put an end to the difficulty by dealing too firmly with the other parent. But this effort is usually resisted, heels are dug in the sand, and just getting along seems an unattainable goal.

At one extreme end of the coparenting continuum are parents who are outright antagonistic, fighting each other in every way imaginable, often putting children in the middle. These coparents use severe language to describe each other's behavior and say they "can't stand" or "hate" one another. They use the court or social service agencies to punish or condemn whenever they can, and they seem to get pleasure out of making each other miserable. Problems only get worse when a new stepparent joins in a system like this and agrees that his or her spouse is the "right" or "better" parent.

At the other end of the cooperation continuum are parents who have mastered the art of working together respectfully, and of being non-judgmental and flexible with each other. In contrast to those who fight, these parents use positive or neutral language when talking about one another, and, while they are neither friends nor lovers, they care about each others' feelings. Individuals who wed a cooperative divorced parent are more likely to support the crossparent in the other home, because they marry into an atmosphere of mutual respect.

•

Between the two extremes are coparents who parallel parent. These former spouses no longer need to be openly hostile because they have no contact with each other, but they still hang onto their rigid beliefs about the other's perceived flaws and shortcomings. Experts find that the children of these coparents are better off because they are out of the line of fire of parents who once fought relentlessly. But these children will still suffer because they still cannot enjoy harmony in the world of the family.

The lesson of the coparenting continuum is that parents who love their children will integrate new partners with the intention of learning to work together as a team. They will not allow new spouses to split them further from the other parent, and they will commit to a goal of cooperation. Even when conflict is high, and even when parallel parenting as a strategy is necessary in the short run, they will continue to strive to cooperate in the long run.

Communication Basics

Ninety percent of divorcing spouses name poor communication as one reason for the demise of the relationship. Yet 75 percent of separated spouses recouple with someone new within only a few years, and most move on without considering how they might communicate better. After remarriage by one or both former spouses, the need for productive communication increases dramatically. The predicament is that the majority of coparents, stepparents and crossparents have few effective skills for communicating at the time in life when they need them the very most.

Good communication begins with the use of manners and language that invites a dialogue.

As I pointed out in Chapter 2, good communication begins with the use of manners and language that invites a dialogue. But successful exchange of thoughts and ideas for the purpose of making decisions requires more than language and tact.

Coparents and new stepparents need to ask for what they want in ways that will be accepted by each other or by parents in the other home. This means learning how to bring up issues in a productive, non-confrontational way.

The Polite Request

Expanding upon the traditional "I message" taught by communication counselors, psychologist P. Leslie Herold recommends using the format of the *polite request* to teach parents who live apart to talk to each other in a helpful way. Here we expand on the idea again to teach all parenting figures in both homes to use this skill. The concept involves expressing your own feelings about a situation before you ask a spouse or coparent for what you want or need. The key is that anger, blame and accusatory tones are never acceptable when making a polite request.

Study the examples below to see how an exchange between crossparents can fail or succeed, depending on the form of the request.

Example 1

> A stepmother: *Now that I'm married to your ex, I want you to get the children to school earlier in the morning. You don't even care about their education!*

> Her crossparent: *How do you know what I care about? You're not even their parent, and you have no right to butt in!*

Conversations like this can only create hostility between the children's mother and new stepmother, and will block any progress in the crossparent relationship.

The key is that anger, blame and accusatory tones are never acceptable when making a polite request.

Example 2

A stepmother: *I worry about the kids' being able to settle down and concentrate when they get to school just in time for the bell to ring. I wonder if we could agree to get them here a few minutes earlier when each of us is in charge of the morning transportation. Do you think we could do that?*

Her crossparent: *OK. I agree that the children need time to get ready to focus and I have noticed that we've been rushed in the mornings. I appreciate your concern and I'll make the effort to be earlier.*

Free of accusation and judgement, a request made out of legitimate concern will usually be well received.

Unlike the first conversation, this exchange will build good will between the children's mother and stepmother. Free of accusation and judgement, a request made out of legitimate concern will usually be well received, and often will be granted. Notice that the mother in the example above did not become defensive and deny that she is sometimes late in the morning, or attack the stepmother for bringing up her concern. Sometimes it helps to rehearse your style of interaction ahead of time, to be ready to react without judgement. Chapter 5 contains more detailed ideas about the basics of productive communication.

Home-to-Home Negotiation

During the first two years of stepfamily life, stress is usually high in the newly formed household and also in dealings with the other home. To a large extent this is normal, and knowing there are tendencies for problems should make you be more patient in learning to handle them. No counselor will tell you it is easy, but most will tell you that you can master the art

The businesslike strategy for calm, thoughtful settlement of issues is by far the most productive approach to use with parents in both households.

of coparenting across two homes if you try. The specific techniques for negotiation outlined in this section apply during all stages of a reorganized family.

Divorced coparents who have learned the procedures of the business approach before they move on may have already worked out ways to negotiate and make compromises between them. Now that they are married again, they also will be using the procedures within their own homes as well, to contract with the new spouse or children on discipline and behavioral issues. The businesslike strategy for calm, thoughtful settlement of issues is by far the most productive approach to use with parents in both households.

Once again it is helpful to remember the advantages of waiting to remarry after divorce. Coparents who learn to negotiate themselves before they bring in other adults will have the strongest scaffolding for building a bigger network. Then, by extending the concept of the business relationship to include new spouses and partners, remarried parents can use the tools of problem solving to achieve a sense of cooperation the fastest. The steps to negotiation presented below can be practiced and refined by parents and stepparents in both homes. When children are aware their parents are working on learning to deal with their other caretakers successfully, they are given the message that their world is composed.

Identify the Problem First
Before any problem can be solved it needs to be defined, and in second-marriage families difficulties arise within and between the homes. The first step in addressing any issue is to determine whether parents in the new household should take on the problem themselves, or whether parents in the other

household should be involved. An easy analysis of the issue will help you decide.

Four kinds of problems can be identified:

1. Problems between coparent and new partner that do not involve the children. These issues might concern matters of money, spending time together, working outside the home, dealing with in-laws and extended family, intimacy and sex, or making holiday plans. Problems that belong to spouses only are problems within the home which can and should be worked out by just the two of you.

2. Problems between the children's coparents that do not directly involve new spouses or the children. These issues might surround matters of child support, setting up schedules, transportation between the homes, school conferences and participation, activity sign-ups and arrangements, medical and counseling issues, or questions about religious participation. These important shared-parenting matters are issues between the coparents, and they should be worked out by the mother and father of the child involved. New spouses and significant others do not take direct part in negotiating these kinds of problems between coparents, but rather inform the new spouse as to their opinions.

3. Problems with children in either household that affect primarily one home. Issues here might involve house rules for children to follow, behavioral expectations, and how consequences are delivered. Matters like homework, chores, bedtimes, and spending time with friends would be common examples. Child issues primarily within the home should be negotiated by parents in the household, using family meetings

This very structured procedure is imperative to use when emotions of the parents are high.

to get the input of the children. Children of divorce are able to adjust to separate sets of expectations in their homes, provided they are not drastically different.

4. Problems with a child's development that are serious, which concern character or emotional growth, and which impact the child's functioning in both homes, school, or the community. Problems of serious depression or acting out fall into this category, as do issues with serious lying, stealing, substance abuse, school failure, or targeting a stepfamily member with aggression.

These problems that exist both *within and between* homes need to be addressed by all parenting partners in both homes. However, totally joint negotiations are only successful when the business approach has been effectively fine-tuned, and when crossparents as well as coparents can work together well. In most cases there will be meetings within each home attended by parents in that home, and meetings between homes attended by the biological parents of the child at risk. This very structured procedure is imperative to use when emotions of the parents are high. Inappropriately involving a new stepparent will slow down problem resolution, even when the new partner's judgement and intentions are good.

Parenting Business Meetings
Some meetings, called coparent business meetings as described in Chapter 1, are attended by just the biological parents of the child. After remarriage, issues within either home should also be addressed in business meetings that we might call spousal meetings. Because difficult feelings may linger for years, though, conjoint business meetings, involving parents and stepparents

in both homes, will happen much less frequently and in many cases never at all. The emotions involved in sitting down to talk with a former spouse's new mate are often just too much to take. Forcing a conjoint meeting of the four of you will fail when feelings cannot be controlled.

Remember that in order to do the best for your children you want to set up a forum that will be successful whenever you need to address a problem. If you are in doubt as to which parenting partners should be involved, analyze the problem again. Coparent meetings between a child's natural mother and father are much less stressful than meetings that all four of you attend, and these conferences are always appropriate. Spousal meetings can follow in both households to advance the problem-solving efforts.

You want to set up a forum that will be successful whenever you need to address a problem.

Steps to Negotiation

Once you have decided which members of the parenting network will sit down together to discuss a problem, use a step-by-step system to generate a plan of action. Business meetings within or between homes are not arenas for fighting, but rather they are places where ideas and opinions are welcome as part of a structured procedure. The value of the following blueprint for negotiation is that structure takes guesswork out of how to begin solving a problem.

☑ *Step 1. Name the problem.* Even though you are already aware of the reason you are getting together to talk, it helps to identify the problem again, to orient yourselves appropriately and make sure everyone is on the same page.

☑   *Step 2. Give opinions and reflect ideas.* Here you may use "reflective listening" as discussed in Chapter 1. Each of you should summarize how the other feels about the problem before you try to generate solutions. When three or four of you are meeting this step may take longer, but it is important that every adult feels understood.

☑   *Step 3. Brainstorm solutions.* In this step you and the other parent or stepparent make lists of all the possible ways to address the issue at hand. One key element in brainstorming is that people may offer ideas without fear of being ridiculed or criticized. Brainstorming is a powerful skill that makes partners more aware that there are usually many solutions to problems. This step builds flexibility into the negotiation procedure.

☑   *Step 4. Choose a solution.* Here the art of compromise meets its test. Parties who are negotiating select the best possible alternative together. This may feel like "giving in" to one parent or the other, but sometimes yielding is the best course of action. If you are usually the more reasonable partner in the business relationship, you should consider accepting an idea of the other partner whenever you are able to see the merit of the plan. Parents who "stick to their guns" just for the sake of prevailing are not doing all they can to compromise.

☑   *Step 5. Take action.* Review what you are agreeing to do to address the issue. It is vital to include a time frame, assign responsibilities to each of you, and set up a future negotiation meeting to re-evaluate the problem.

☑ *Step 6. Review and re-assess.* At a designated time, talk to each other about whether there has been progress in working out the problem. Decide together whether you should repeat the negotiation process or whether you have resolved the issue.

All adults who practice the basics of meeting to negotiate solutions to problems will do better than those who do not learn to use organized strategies. In families where multiple marriages have occurred, the techniques of talking and listening well and of learning to negotiate are invaluable. Mental health experts agree that adding structure almost always lowers anxiety about stressful situations, and in cases where the fundamental well-being of your children is at stake, the steps you take to communicate are critical.

Learning to Keep Commitments

Many problems develop when divorced coparents fail to keep commitments they have negotiated with each other. Courts require that parenting plans be developed which detail arrangements for care of children, and most mothers and fathers sign these documents willingly. Unfortunately, divorce agreements are too often broken by angry or grieving coparents who do not remain true to their word.

Divorce agreements are too often broken by angry or grieving coparents who do not remain true to their word.

Statements like the following result:

- ◆ *He's always late dropping off the children.*
- ◆ *She never lets me know when she's going out of town.*
- ◆ *His agreements mean absolutely nothing.*

After remarriage the mistake of failing to carry out responsibilities can even worsen. New partners who disapprove of the former spouse may discourage the child's parent from carefully complying with plans, or the biological parent in a new relationship may become further entrenched in a belief that the other coparent is unreasonable. When one parent recouples leaving the other still single, non-compliance becomes a way to object to the former spouse's remarriage. In many cases the coping mechanism of passive resistance is at play. In efforts to be assertive with the other parent, former partners send a message that they simply will not be controlled or told what to do.

- *Her new husband tells her to ignore my telephone messages.*
- *Since he remarried he won't even talk to me.*

The simple message here is that when coparents, stepparents, or crossparents fail to keep their commitments to each other, they let the children down. Violating parenting plans to target another parent becomes a poor coping device when it hurts the children you love. Passive resistance only escalates conflict. Parents who rationalize their behavior by offering various explanations for their stubbornness should understand that they are putting their own needs before those of the children. There are few legitimate excuses for ignoring the most important premise of parenting after divorce: *keep the children's needs first.*

Coparents and significant others should develop the habit of keeping commitments they make for the sake of the children. This means following written agreements carefully, remembering to review the plans, and communicating with each other whenever you need to change them.

- *I need to change the drop-off time for the children. Could we talk about that?*
- *I'd like to schedule a trip of my own. When can we discuss the schedule?*

Trust may be the most important quality of any business association, but it is absolutely crucial for making life happy for children in two homes. Parents who can rely on each other's integrity will gain mutual respect, which is at the center of the coparenting relationship.

Yours, Mine, and Ours

Just as the parenting network enlarges when one or both parents remarry, so does the network of children. In some families the biological girl or boy of one spouse will remain the only child, but in many there will be more children. When a divorced parent remarries someone else with children, there are stepsiblings in the home. Children have stepsiblings in both of their homes when each of their parents remarries someone else with children. Some of these child relationships may be full-time, but others will be part-time as children transition to their other homes on different schedules. Problems of jealousy and resentment between stepchildren are almost universal, especially in the first two years.

Many newlywed spouses naturally desire to have another child together. Perhaps as part of the need to create a feeling of "us" which is unique to life after remarriage, one or both partners yearn for a child of their own. When this new child is born, the stepchildren have a new half-sibling and the child network grows again. The birth of the baby brings joy to the parents, but it brings more complications to the family.

The former spouse of a remarried parent may have trouble dealing with the fact that a once intimate lover now has a child with someone else. When there was conflict in the coparenting relationship to begin with, feelings of disapproval and further abandonment may emerge. A child is tangible evidence that a former partner has a new family to love. The parent who now has two sets of children may be accused of favoring those in the second family, and sometimes this may be the case. Other times, as children grow older, they can appear to take on traits of the disgruntled outside coparent, and can lose the affection of the parent with a new child.

Children in serial families are given substantial challenges when they acquire stepsiblings. When a new baby is born, a child may have even more difficulty. Now he or she must share a parent with a sibling whose other parent "belongs" to a step-sister or brother. A boy or girl who may have felt secure about the love of the natural parent may begin to question that love. Older children may even reject the baby and shift loyalty to the other home.

To address these complications, coparents and stepparents need to be attentive to their children's feelings and patiently help them adjust. By far the most important tool is reflective listening, as introduced in Chapter 1. Girls and boys with care-takers who are able to draw out their many mixed feelings get a message of understanding and love. Working with them to make each one feel special takes enormous effort, but it is with this kind of family work that parents keep their children their first priority.

The birth of the baby brings joy to the parents, but it brings more complications to the family.

Parents in second marriages who combine and build families will need to put the needs of all the children first. Ideas are presented in the following section for deciding how to meet those needs. Chapter 7 will outline strategies for solving common problems with children and for helping them grow into happy adults.

Balance as a Goal

Two words describe happy stepfamilies: flexible and balanced. Both concepts imply that stepparents and stepchildren have found ways to live without rigidity. Each family member gets enough of what she or he needs to feel satisfied, and each acknowledges that the other parents and children need the same thing.

The Pie-Chart of Personal Needs
This simple graphic can be used as a tool for deciding how to address the needs of each family member. For every child and adult, important parts of family life are diagrammed as slices of a pie, and this pie might be thought of as the individual's inter-personal world. The size of each slice represents the degree of importance each relationship has to the person in question, and gives us an idea about how much time and attention should be given to that relationship. Sometimes the need is to spend one-on-one time with a parent or stepparent, and other times the need is to spend time together as a family unit.

Consider the pie-charts of two hypothetical children; Child A in her father's home and Child B in his mother's home.

Child A's Needs   **Child B's Needs**

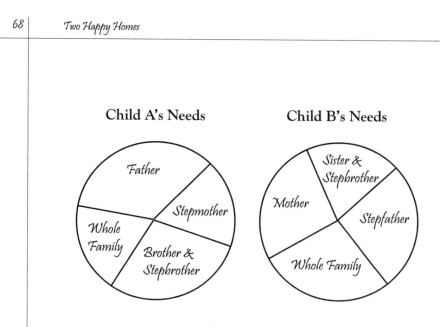

Child A needs quite a bit of time and attention from her father, perhaps because she is still very young. This child's father and stepmother will arrange for her to have lots of one-on-one time with her father whenever she is with them. Child B, in contrast, needs more time with his new stepparent, possibly because his biological father is not very involved with him. This boy's mother and stepfather will arrange for him to have one-on-one time with each of them, and he will also spend time with his siblings and with the whole family together.

To use the pie-chart idea with your stepfamily, first try to determine how much time and attention each of your children need with each of you, how much they need with each other, and how much they need to be with the family as a whole. Next, make plans that will balance out the needs of all your children as best you can. Although Child B above needed a good deal of attention from his stepfather, this situation is actually quite rare. Most stepchildren do not want or need to spend as much time with a stepparent as they do with the biological parent. New spouses and partners should be flexible and tolerant when children need individual time with a parent. Partners who find themselves feeling worried or jealous when natural parents spend one-on-one time with a child should resort to reframing as a coping skill. Telling yourself that a child needs *a larger slice of the pie* with a biological parent will help, because this is the case in almost every new stepfamily.

Second families get along the best when all combinations of family members are at some time the focus of time and attention. Each parent should spend time with each, and all, of his or her own children, apart from the stepparent or stepchildren. Other times the children should all be together with both parents, though this slice of time may need to be briefer if the children are in conflict. It is also important to study each adult's pie-chart of personal needs. Many remarried men and women simply need time alone. Spouses also need time together to make certain to attend to their relationship as a couple. Balancing the needs of each child and parent can be difficult, especially when some children are in the home part-time while others live there most or all of the time.

Combining flexibility with balance means recognizing that there are many ways to fill needs once you have identified them. Try not to overreact if your spouse spends money on his or her child, and try not to be competitive yourself by lavishing your own child with material things. Remember that love and attention are the things that matter, and there are many ways of giving children quality time. Young children will feel special if one-on-one time just means a game at the dining room table, and older children will be gratified when a parent gives them

> *Combining flexibility with balance means recognizing that there are many ways to fill needs once you have identified them.*

transportation to a friend's house. Longer outings or activities are beneficial, but when they are hard to schedule because needs seem to be in conflict, use flexibility and creativity in making the moments happen.

The bottom line is that the important tasks of stepparents, coparents and crossparents are ongoing until the children are grown, and once the family has been formed there is no choice but to keep on parenting. If all of you maintain balance as your goal and flexibility as your way of attaining equilibrium, you will have the best chance of filling everyone's needs.

Chapter 4

TEN PROBLEM PATTERNS

Certainly no two combined family systems are entirely alike. Fortunately though, human behavior tends to be repetitive, and patterns of problems develop. The scenarios in this chapter depict common situations after remarriage by one or both divorced coparents. Although they are hypothetical, they contain elements of family dynamics that develop every day. If these circumstances seem familiar, you may be able to avoid trouble for your family by gaining a better understanding of how common problems develop.

First look for your own behavior as you read through the following examples. Try to be honest with yourself and make changes if you should, for the good of all family members. Next, think about whether your spouse, former spouse, or another family member fits into a problem pattern. Then, for the sake of your children, read the messages of advice after each situation. Using skills of communication like those I outlined in Chapter 3, do what you can to keep a troublesome chain of events from plaguing your family.

Pattern 1. Coparents Prolong Negative Intimacy

After years of trying to make a difficult marriage work, you are forced to go through with divorce. One or both of you always had a fiery temper and often started arguments, but now that you are separated things are worse than ever. Other divorced parents seem able to work together, but your situation just does not improve. Angry disagreements escalate to hostile arguments over money, past problems, and issues with the children. Even after one of you remarries, there is absolutely no relief, and an almost violent quality continues to pervade your life. Both of you know you each love the children, but you seem to hold onto the hate for each other.

Negative intimacy is the Number One issue for divorced parents to deal with.

Negative intimacy is the Number One issue for divorced parents to deal with. Spouses who related to each other with conflict during their marriage are those most likely to continue in conflict for years, and far too many do. As I discussed in Chapter 1, this is because negative intimacy became the basis of your bond while you were together, and fighting became a habit. With the additional stress of grief after divorce, there is no foundation for a positive alliance, or even a neutral relationship. Though it seems to be a contradiction, negative attachment is very strong. When stepparents marry into a coparenting system like this, they are usually unable to change the dynamics, and can even add fuel to the fire.

Message:

If you are a separated spouse and you find yourself still reaching out to your former wife or husband in anger, stop and ask yourself if you are automatically overreacting. In situations where you are the partner who is constantly criticized or pursued, try to respond with less emotion. Both of you should practice disengaging from each other by making yourselves wait longer before making phone calls, and by letting time go by before you respond.

Instead of: *It's just like you to forget to give our son the medicine! You only care about yourself! You always were selfish, and I guess you always will be.*

Try: *I'll try to remember how busy you are. I know you care about our son just as much as I do. Next time I'll be sure to remind you about the medicine.*

Former spouses who know each other well can use their knowledge about each other in hurtful ways. Venting feelings may feel good for the moment, but the effect on the relationship is only destructive in the long term. To eliminate negative intimacy from how you relate to each other, stay in touch about your parenting concerns, avoid pushing each other's buttons, and temper your comments with neutrality.

Pattern 2. Bitterness After An Affair

Married for several years and after your son or daughter has started school, your spouse leaves you for a younger woman or man. This individual had an affair with your spouse during the marriage, and your separation was traumatic. Feeling betrayed, scorned, and alone, you throw yourself into parenthood, cling to the children who love you, and have trouble moving on with your life. Even when you someday remarry, your intense hostility remains directed at your former spouse, the man or woman who broke up your family, or both. Unfortunately for you, anger and unresolved grief serve as a permanent barrier to the final stage in resolving grief — acceptance.

Deceived parents can meet this ultimate challenge by learning to deal with reality head on, and by separating their feelings from their behavior.

While prolonged negative intimacy may be the most common problem stopping coparents from recovering from divorce, overcoming the damage of an affair is often the most difficult. Developing trust for one who has insulted your integrity may be impossible, and without trust, parenting well cannot happen. But deceived parents can meet this ultimate challenge by learning to deal with reality head on, and by separating their feelings from their behavior. Though you may continue to feel resentment for your former spouse or the person he or she married, your civil and tempered behavior will show your children how much you love them.

Message:

Children who live with a parent still furious because of betrayal will suffer immensely. Sometimes the rejected father or mother goes for years in utter rage, unable to move on or demonstrate any kind of acceptance. If you recognize yourself in this position, try using "self talk" to work on your grief. Ask yourself questions that will help you see your self-worth, and tell yourself that life will go on.

- *Is life really all that bad?*
- *Is this the worst that could happen?*
- *I know I'm a very good parent.*
- *I know I can go on with life.*
- *I know life will be good again.*

Rebuffed men and women who withdraw into self-pity or actively campaign for revenge are certain to create misery for themselves as well as their children. To show the greatest love of all for your son or daughter, commit yourself to getting past this greatest of personal insults.

Pattern 3. The Overprotective Coparent

Now it is time to move on with your life, and you take the step to remarry. Still feeling guilt about your children going through divorce, however, you bring a cautious spirit to your marriage and unconsciously limit your new partner's role. In the interest of "making it up" to your children, you remarry to complete the family constellation, but then discourage and even disallow your new spouse from becoming involved. Overemphasizing the importance of coparenting with your former spouse, you construct rigid boundaries between your child and the new adult in the family. As a result, your child never bonds with the stepparent, your partner feels left out, and your family feels artificial.

Loving coparents who operate in ways that prevent growth in the stepfamily unit can sow the seeds for a second failed marriage. Two unfortunate dynamics interfere. First, your child will remain distant from an adult who could have loved your boy or girl and helped you with the parenting. Worse yet, over time your spouse may resent your child, and even you, because of the exclusion.

Message:

Once you have decided to move on and remarry, the reality of a new family life is upon you. Try not to let fear and shame for the past control how you shape the style of your family. Talk

Try not to let fear and shame for the past control how you shape the style of your family.

with your partner and with your coparent in the other home about how to tap into the strengths of each of them. Your child will be the happiest if he or she gets the benefit of a positive stepparent relationship *and* keeps a close and wonderful alliance with the natural parent.

> **Statement of a happy child:**
> *My mom and dad both love me, and I have neat stepparents too. Even though I feel closer to my parents, I know all of them are there for me. I really have a great family!*

Pattern 4. The Overinvolved Stepparent

Although you have no children of your own, you have learned to love your new spouse's sons or daughters, and you want the best for them. Someday you may or may not have a natural child in the marriage, but for now you are delighted to be totally involved with your stepchildren. Taking naturally to motherhood or fatherhood, you work very hard to fill the demands of becoming a great stepparent to the children, and to get them to love you back. At first you feel fulfilled and your spouse loves you all the more for your effort, but the child's parent in the other home seems to feel jealous and possessive. In spite of the strengths in your marital bond, the task of parenting the children in cooperation with the other parent becomes disastrous. Soon you cannot talk to your stepchild's other parent at all; you become the target of his or her anger, and your spouse is caught in the middle.

The example above illustrates what can happen when a stepparent enters the family too eager to become involved. Another common problem develops when the stepparent is pushed or prodded into overinvolvement by the child's biological parent, as though to replace the original parent in the other home. Sometimes this happens out of a separated parent's failure to see that each child's birthparents will always be most important, and that parents are never replaced by stepparents. It also can happen out of an angry coparent's spite and anger toward the former partner, however, and this dynamic is very hurtful. A child who is encouraged to accept a replacement parent becomes confused about his or her identity, and the biological parent in the other home becomes upset.

The crossparent relationship is doomed when an overenthusiastic stepparent steps in too quickly, too often, or with too much energy. It is natural for the child's original parent to be territorial about the child's world. Stepmothers especially are perceived as intrusive when they appear as too involved with a boy or girl the crossparent has raised since birth. If you are a stepparent in the first years of remarriage, your wisest move is to respect the primary parent relationship, and wait until later to take a more active role. Bond with your stepchild one-on-one, but leave the home-to-home parenting to your spouse.

Message:
In this case, specific advice for everyday happenings may help you out the most. Don't ask or tell your stepchild to call you "dad" or "mom." Don't "be helpful" by changing a child's appearance — getting haircuts or ear piercings, or purchasing extreme clothing. Leave decisions about Halloween costumes and birthday parties to the child's natural parents. Milestone

A child who is encouraged to accept a replacement parent becomes confused about his or her identity.

Children who lose a parent after divorce may be worse off than those who lose a parent through death.

events and many holiday moments are still personal between children and their mothers and fathers, especially in the first two years of remarried life.

Pattern 5. A Grieving Parent Drops Out

After struggling so long with the pain of divorce and now the remarriage of your former spouse, life is very hard. Battles with your coparent and crossparent are endless, and they take a tremendous toll. Although you love your children, things have become almost unbearable. Slowly you cave in to battle fatigue and decrease your participation, paying minimal attention to your child, and letting your coparent "win." You still grieve the losses of divorce daily, but at least this way you can survive, with or without a spouse of your own.

Too often parents are discouraged from staying involved and drop out of the lives of their children. Struggles over money, parenting time, and everyday issues with the children are hard enough to take, but when these are coupled with ongoing disapproval and criticism, many hurting mothers and fathers go their separate ways. Some find reasons to move to another city or state and justify this by thinking "it's better for the children." But rarely is it really better for a parent to give up, even when coparenting is very difficult. Studies suggest that children who lose a parent after divorce may be worse off than those who lose a parent through death.

Messages:

To a parent dropping out: Stop, reconsider your actions, and rethink what the effect will be on your child. See what you can do to stay involved, and connect with people who can give you ideas. If your situation dictates a move away, figure out ways to remain in touch, for example using cell phones and computers. Counselors tell us that children who see or talk with parents *infrequently but consistently* are much better off than those who have unpredictable contact or none at all.

To the former spouse: Do what you can to encourage your child's other parent to remain involved. Arrange for contact even when there are serious financial problems, and when overnight parenting time cannot take place. Keep in mind that even short but consistent times spent together will reassure your daughter or son of the parent's love. Work with your remarried partner as well, and go out of your way in the interest of preventing further loss for your child.

Pattern 6. The Opinionated Crossparent

As a new spouse, you believe one of your responsibilities is to support your partner in dealing with the other coparent. After hearing the reasons for the divorce and observing your crossparent at exchanges with the children, you can see why the first marriage had to end. You conclude that this individual has many problems and seems to be very disturbed. Soon you believe that your new home is by far the healthier one and feel frustrated that you and your spouse are required to work with a hopeless individual. Your crossparent also complains about you, however, and tells friends and neighbors that you are trying to run things. Neither of you respects the way the other operates and, in a word, the situation is miserable.

Natural parents who are threatened by the former spouse's new chosen partner can construct impossible hurdles.

New spouses often "take up the sword" for the person they marry, intending to help. Perhaps believing that disapproval of the former spouse will make them a better husband or wife, they escalate conflict by interfering too aggressively. Suspicious that a positive coparenting relationship between the children's mother and father will mean less love for them, insecure stepparents can build barriers between the homes. Conversely, natural parents who are threatened by the former spouse's new chosen partner also can construct impossible hurdles.

Messages:

To the stepparent: Watch out for signs that you are making matters worse. When your spouse complains about the other parent, ask questions to probe for reality.

- *Is he really all that bad?*
- *Could you be overreacting?*

Consider that your crossparent may be acting out only because of stress, and question your own reactions.

- *Is there a reason she could be so upset?*
- *Am being too critical here?*

Don't be afraid to admit mistakes, and apologize when you have erred. Raising children in two-home families is very difficult, and all members of the parenting battery can expect to make mistakes.

To the parent: Try to be tolerant of the new stepparent's enthusiasm for the job. Remind yourself that you will always be the primary parent to your children, and reassure yourself that you will never be replaced. Fight back urges to "put her in her place" or "tell him where to go" because these actions will aggravate rather than help.

Children of divorce and remarriage are just innocent bystanders when clashes between parenting figures occur.

Children of divorce and remarriage are just innocent bystanders when clashes between parenting figures occur. Boys and girls almost universally tell therapists they "wish their families could get along," so your task is to strive for harmony.

Pattern 7. The Overpunitive Stepparent

Even before the wedding, your new spouse's child didn't like you. Your growing love for your partner, though, made you decide you could cope with the stress. But in the months after the wedding, your stepchild grew more difficult, acting out and disobeying both of you. Disrespect is hard to tolerate. Stepping in to stop the defiance, you get louder, harsher, even physical with your stepchild. After several ugly incidents, the child seems entrenched in hate.

Two forces are at work in this scene. First, the child is having trouble accepting the remarriage of a parent, and acting up is a child's way of expressing grief. The second dynamic is the new spouse's impatience with conflict caused by the child. Men and women who marry a coparent with a grieving child will need to be very patient. Try not to allow yourself to become trapped in your own anger.

Message:

Perhaps the hottest topic in stepfamilies is discipline of the children. This issue will be addressed in Chapter 7, but specific caution is appropriate here. Stepparents should almost always avoid punishing the children of a spouse, for several very good reasons. First, the child will resent your "taking over" the role of disciplinarian, and may reject your efforts to build a relationship. Your crossparent in the other home is sure to object if you are harsh, and your working relationship will be jeopar-

The most frequent reason families after divorce and remarriage seek help is inappropriate treatment of the children.

dized. Even worse, your spouse will be anxious and worried, and may begin to question the marriage.

Experts report that the most frequent reason families seek help after divorce and remarriage is inappropriate treatment of the children.

When in Doubt, Don't......discipline your spouse's child.

Pattern 8. The Underinvolved Stepparent.

Before your second marriage, you and your new partner read books about becoming a stepfamily. Believing that blending your children would be tricky, you wisely searched for advice. The books warned about difficulties in stepfamily life and suggested that each of you be in charge of your own children. Each of you focused on your own offspring, and this way of living seemed to work. Now several years have gone by, though, and your stepchild is having serious problems. Because you never really bonded, your efforts to help are rejected. Your stepchild alleges you were "never there before," and has trouble believing you are concerned.

Stepparents who do not bond with a stepchild in the early years find it difficult to help later on when issues arise. Since mutual caring and trust never developed, there is no basis on which to intervene. Here the child's biological parent must deal with the problem alone, without direct help from a spouse. Even after years of living together in a stepfamily, there will be feelings of isolation when relationships have not developed.

Message:

Similar to the message in Pattern 3, the best advice to a new stepparent is to get involved in the life of your new stepchild, at a pace that is best for the child. Read Chapter 2 again and decide whether you are an acquaintance, friend, or a more intimate caring adult to the child. Don't be afraid to move ahead and take steps to deepen the bond, but be sure to talk to your spouse about your intentions.

As in any important relationship, communication is an essential key. Stepmoms and stepdads who are tentative about entering a stepchild's life will benefit from a reminder that *reflective listening* is the key to having a child feel understood by any caring adult.

Get involved in the life of your new stepchild, at a pace that is best for the child.

This simple sequence illustrates how a child will accept your gesture to become more involved:

Child: *I don't think I want any dinner.*

Stepparent: *I guess you're not hungry.*

Child: *It's just that I don't feel good.*

Stepparent: *Can you tell me what's wrong?*

Child: *I miss my other home.*

Stepparent: *Oh, let's talk about what we can do.*

Child: *OK.*

To avoid being left out as an effective stepparent, take advantage of opportunities to help your stepchild by being ready to listen.

Holding on too tightly at the beginning and trying to force a fit will fail.

Two Ways Families Try Too Hard

Pattern 9. The Overstructured Stepfamily.

You and your new spouse are determined to succeed in your second marriage. While engaged you get the children together to talk about forming one family out of two. Because they are close in age, you want them to be friends, and you tell them to accept each other. As responsible future spouses you make concerted efforts to be proactive, and you explain to the children that you are going to be a well-run family. After the wedding, determined to get things right in this marriage, you follow tenets of court-ordered plans with your former spouses exactly. To control conflict with the outside coparents you communicate as infrequently as possible, avoiding intrusion and focusing on your own new family.

Not long after the wedding, though, serious issues develop. The children haven't meshed as well as you intended, and they refuse to refer to each other as "brother" and "sister." Each of them has refused to bond with their stepparent, and coordinating things with the other two homes has become impossible. You rarely have all your children together, and when you do, it feels odd and unnatural. As parenting partners, you and your spouse now argue about issues with the children, and you can't function as the team you started out to be. Things are very disordered and, as a family, you are unhappy.

The boundaries in this hurting family are too rigid, both within and between the homes. Holding on too tightly at the beginning and trying to force a fit will fail. Even when both recoupled spouses agree completely about the kind of family they want, children can drive a wedge between them by opposing all their efforts. And parents in the other home can resist the push by withdrawing from collaboration.

Message:

A critical concept presented in Chapter 2 was that hopes for happiness in stepfamilies are often dashed when spouses try to create the perfect family. Remember that your new family will go through several stages before you reach your real level of comfort, and your unique family identity will be different from what you expected. During the process you will need to be patient, tolerant and flexible, and always be ready to change.

Pattern 10. The Understructured Stepfamily

Not wanting to force strict rules or expectations on the children, you and your new spouse decide on a relaxed approach. Confused about what second families are supposed to look like, you adopt a wait and see attitude. At first this style feels right, and you describe your parenting as "laid back." But after a while, problems begin to pop up as children start to squabble about bedrooms, toys, and clothing. Patiently trying to work with the children, you put out fires as they start. Soon you begin to step on each other's toes about discipline, though, and each of you comes down hard on the other's children. What started out feeling comfortable now feels all wrong.

To rectify the problem, you and your spouse decide on affirmative action. You sit down to write family rules and consequences, and present them to the children. You are met with outrage and resistance to this change, which the children see as unfair. One or two of the children begin to act out seriously, and things become even worse. Demands for a reduction of time in your home come from the coparent in a child's other home. A rift develops between the two of you, and the new marriage is now in jeopardy.

Message:

Whether you are a parent contemplating a second family or a parent in trouble with the family you have, setting *balance* as

Using the format of the parent business meeting, sit down with your spouse in a relaxed setting and try to work out a flexible plan.

your goal will help you set up a structure that will work. Using the format of the parent business meeting, sit down with your spouse in a relaxed setting and try to work out a flexible plan.

Even if you have already tried writing down how issues like chores and consequences for behavior will be handled, you will have to try again. First make an inventory of the needs of each family member, as discussed in Chapter 3, then write out ways those needs can be met. Be specific enough that each family member knows what to do, and what will happen when things go wrong. It may take another family meeting with the children as well, not to lay down the rules, but to get their input and find out how they feel. When children are resistant to having meetings, as adolescents often are, have a briefer meeting or take their input by proxy, asking them for their vote on ideas without their attending the session. Be sure to get back to the children when household decisions have been made, and be sure to tell them there will be follow-up meetings.

When strategies to structure the family have failed, parents should go back to the drawing board. Review what you have been doing and decide to make a change. One or both of you may be able to get suggestions from a former spouse, or you may need to consult a counselor who routinely helps divorced coparents and stepparents. Either way, your continuing drive to make your family thrive is your continuing responsibility. Family management is an ongoing task until the children are grown.

Remember that your happiness as a married couple depends on the quality of your personal relationship and on the depth of your commitment to each other. Part of the promise you make in tying the knot is to hang in and cope with the inevitable challenges of stepfamily life. While the phrase *parents are forever* may describe the viewpoint of the children, *families are forever* should describe yours.

The Stepfamily Parenting Plan

A strategy as simple as writing out your intentions for parenting in your stepfamily at the time of your marriage may help you avoid many of the problems described in this chapter. Separated mothers and fathers are required to file plans for parenting when they complete the process of divorce because the court wants to know their intentions. Parents who remarry might consider doing the same thing but for other reasons.

Crafting a stepfamily parenting plan will help you move toward a complete and healthy separation from your former partners. Defining the responsibilities of each adult will also help you organize the division of labor in areas of parenting in your new home. Writing out how you intend to deal with issues will give you guidance when questions arise about how to approach things. Perhaps most important, going through the motions of formalizing a written plan will encourage you both to *think through* how you intend to structure your stepfamily, and life will be better because you did.

A Sample Plan
The plan on the following pages illustrates how a remarried couple might outline their intentions to build a flexible, balanced family while working together with parents in two other homes.

Writing out how you intend to deal with issues will give you guidance when questions arise about how to approach things.

Our Family Plan

We, John and Jane Doe, plan to combine our families with love, patience, and understanding. We are in agreement that the best interests of our children will be served if we create an atmosphere that provides for the individual needs of Jane's son and John's daughter. We also recognize that each of our children has a parent in another home, and we pledge ourselves to learning to work successfully with them.

Parental Responsibility. Each of us will have primary responsibility for our own child in our home. This means that we will make sure their needs are met, and although we will try to function as a family unit, each of us will defer to the other when an important decision must be made for our own child. We also recognize that each of us will be coparenting with our child's parent in the other home, and we agree to accept this practice.

Parenting Time. Jane's daughter will live with us every other Thursday evening until Monday morning. John's son will live with us every other week. We acknowledge that Jane's daughter will need one-on-one time with Jane because she will be with us less often than John's son. We plan to make efforts to meet the needs of both our children in making the parenting time for each of them happy and loving while they are with us.

Discipline. We agree that each of us will discipline our own child. We will confer about rules of behavior required in our home, and we will give our children written guidelines we expect them to follow. We will strive to have uniform behavioral expectations of our children, but we recognize that this may not be completely possible. We will consider our children's input in setting up these rules about how they treat us and each other, and we will change them as our children grow. We will not be harsh with our children, and neither of us will use physical discipline. We will use logical consequences and withdraw special privileges when punishment is necessary. We will confer with each other frequently, and each of us will take into account the other's opinions about our child. When we continue to disagree about what is best, we will seek counseling.

Household Rules and Chores. We agree that each of our children should have responsibilities in our home. We will set bedtime at 8 p.m. during the school week and at 9:30 p.m. on weekends. Each of us will consult with our child's other parent to coordinate bedtimes in the other home if possible. We agree to change the bedtime hour as our children get older, and with input from the other homes when necessary. Our children will also be expected to keep their rooms reasonably clean, keep toys and belongings neat, help with cleaning on the weekends, and feed our dog. We will set up a schedule for those chores after getting our children's input about them. We agree to change what chores our children are expected to do as they grow.

Working with Parents in Our Children's Other Homes. We agree to respect the other parent of each of our children, and to respect their spouses as well. Each of us will maintain a positive working relationship with our child's other parent, and each of us agrees to support those coparenting relationships. We will not attend the coparent business meetings of each other unless specifically asked to do so. We will strive to connect with our crossparents and support their relationships with our children. We acknowledge the importance of working together across homes so our children can lead happy, carefree lives.

_____   _____
Signature of Jane   **Signature of John**

Even without going so far as to compose and sign a written document, parents who remarry should give much thought to the way they will parent their children. In Chapter 6 I present specific rules and guidelines that parents, stepparents, and crossparents should follow for the welfare of their boys and girls. Chapter 7 addresses the fact that currently mothers and fathers enter *unwritten* contracts for parenting at the outset of both first and second marriages. Only in cases of legal divorce are the intentions of biological parents of children reduced to writing in the form of parenting plans. Perhaps this practice will change as more recoupling men and women decide to formalize plans for combining their families.

Chapter 5

EMPATHY HELPS AND HEALS

The Element of Empathy

As separated parents work at getting past grief and move on to setting up second families, they can benefit from learning certain ways to be effective in their future relationships. Counselors who work with families have found that one key to doing this comes from developing a special kind of understanding.

Empathy is the ability to identify with the feelings of others, to imagine what they experience, and to adapt our reactions in response. It differs from sympathy in that it does not imply we extend pity or sorrow to the other person, only that we understand. Regardless of the specific plan or schedule that is followed after remarriage, the power of empathy in family situations is immense.

Author David Goleman described the development of empathy in his popular book *Emotional Intelligence*. Centuries earlier, though, philosopher David Hume wrote about the idea of

In post-divorce family situations, empathy for a former spouse or for your child's new stepparent is essential.

putting ourselves in someone else's place to gain perspective about how they feel. Even babies react to distress in people around them as if it were discomfort of their own. Encouraged by a parent to understand unpleasant sensations in others, a growing child learns to imagine negative feelings, and acts to relieve another child's pain. Some youngsters later become very empathic individuals, but others, without a sensitive nature or without the early training by parents, do not.

Fortunately, empathy as an ability can be worked on at any age. It takes practice in imagining the feelings of others, and a commitment to keep practicing in the face of difficult circumstances. If you have a problem with empathy or if you know someone who does, the pages that follow will be important. For the sake of the children you love, your decision to strengthen this important ability may lead your family to peace.

Empathic Understanding

Empathy for the Past

By gaining an understanding of your coparent's or crossparent's experience in the past it can be easier to become accepting of current behavior that bothers you. Similar to the skill of *reframing*, developing empathy for someone allows you to adopt a view of that person that is non-judgmental. In post-divorce family situations, empathy for a former spouse or for your child's new stepparent is essential.

Consider some of the problem patterns presented in Chapter 4. In each of these examples, a former spouse or new partner has personal issues because of the past.

Pattern 1: Dealing with negative intimacy. This problem is by far the most common in families that continue in conflict. If you have an annoying former spouse who seems to badger you constantly, try to imagine how he or she feels to have lost daily contact with you through divorce. Even if day-to-day life before the separation was always disagreeable, your spouse learned to depend on that interaction because it provided an emotional connection to you. Your importance to your former mate was immeasurable, and although now most contact is conflictual, it is still important. To some people, a negative relationship is better than no relationship at all, and believe it or not, connecting with you in any way lowers anxiety in your former spouse. Try to remember this as you react to your coparent's "harassment" in ways that do not escalate conflict.

Pattern 2: After an affair. Two points of view are important to understand when a liaison has led to divorce. In order to move on, both spouses should try to empathize with the other's pain, even in the worst scenarios. First, if you are the parent who left your spouse for someone else, try putting yourself in your coparent's place. Feeling rejected, misled, and betrayed, this parent will understandably be angry or hostile. While you may have had good reasons for leaving, an abandoned spouse will always struggle with feelings of desertion and inadequacy.

If you are the stranded spouse though, you have the greatest task of all. It will take extraordinary strength, but your first job is to search inside yourself to find your own contribution to the marital breakdown. By doing this painful inventory, you will gain a broader perspective about why your coparent left, and develop more acceptance. Even if your analysis leads you to the conclusion that you made no real mistake yourself,

It will take extraordinary strength, but your first job is to search inside yourself to find your own contribution to the marital breakdown.

achieving an empathic stance will help. By telling yourself that your former spouse is incapable of long-term commitment, for example, you may become more tolerant, and by understanding that he or she may also feel guilty, you will handle yourself and the new relationship you have with your former spouse even better.

Pattern 3: Understanding overprotection. There are many ways this dynamic affects divorced and remarried parents. Your former spouse may discourage your contact with the children, or your new spouse may not let you get close to your stepchild. Before you let yourself become disappointed or rush to hostile confrontation, though, put yourself in his or her shoes and try to imagine how the overprotective parent feels about having let the children down. Think about the guilt that consumes any divorced parent, who probably made an unspoken promise of foreverness to the children. This parent probably feels like a traitor who has betrayed the young and innocent. Understanding how your spouse or former partner feels, and keeping these feelings in mind, you can gently nudge him or her out of the rut of overprotection.

Empathy for the Long-Term Past
Empathizing with a parent's more distant past can also help separated and recoupled spouses deal with difficult everyday events. Every person's childhood and early life experience greatly affect how they handle the present. Understanding the impact of the past can give you a frame of reference for coping with current struggles and guide you to better management of ongoing incidents.

Understanding the impact of the past can give you a frame of reference for coping with current struggles.

Pattern 4: An overinvolved stepparent. Men and women who marry divorced parents are often so enthusiastic that they overstep their bounds, especially early on. If you are the child's other parent you may believe that your turf has been invaded, and your initial response might be defensive. But finding out a few facts about your child's new stepparent may help you respond more reasonably and more flexibly.

As an example, consider a new stepmother who grew up as an only child in a family where the mother ran off with another man, stranding the father and daughter. This woman, now a caretaker in a family with children, is likely to overplay the role of mother, perhaps to play-out her own unmet need for better care earlier in life. When you look at it this way, the stepmother's habits of hovering around your children and trying to bond too quickly will not seem as offensive.

Pattern 5: Opinionated crossparents. Relating to a parent in the same sex role across households is equally frustrating to coparents and new stepparents. To illustrate, think about a man who is married for the second time to a woman with three lively children. This stepfather develops a pattern of firmly helping his new spouse to "put her foot down" when the children are rowdy. In this man's teenage years he was criticized by his mother for being a weak and disappointing son, and in his first marriage his wife routinely called him an ineffective parent. Determined to do better the second time around, his firm backing in discipline is appreciated by his spouse. The children's natural father at first objects to intrusion by this new stepparent when the children complain that their stepfather "is mean." Upon learning about the crossparent's history in conversations with his former spouse, however, the father begins to empathize more with the stepfather and reacts differently, with much less criticism and blame.

It can be hard for a divorced parent to empathize with the experience of a child's new stepparent, but it can be equally difficult for a new stepmother or father to accept the behavior of a coparent. A new stepmother who observes the children's biological parent neglecting to set up birthday parties for the children which routinely took place before the divorce might overreact and label the coparent "neglectful." After learning that the crossparent was taught as a child to celebrate birthdays without parties or gifts because of a religious belief, however, the response will be more tempered. Many parents revert to habits or teachings of their early years when they separate from a partner who has done things differently. Now able to empathize with the feelings of the children's natural parent, the new stepmother in this situation will be more understanding.

Pattern 6: The case of the dropout parent. Perhaps the most painful situation occurs when a biological parent develops apathy for parenting. Research shows that children out of contact with parents have a poor prognosis for healthy development. Understanding how or why this perceived disinterest occurs can help. In the following case, there is pain inflicted on a child by abandonment, but it is eased by an empathic parent and his mate.

A divorced mother who had been beaten and raped as a young girl ceased paying child support and stopped calling or seeing her son. She eventually moved out of the country after her child's father remarried. The stepmother stepped in, willingly, with both financial and emotional support. When the child grieved the loss of his mother, both dad and new stepmom

Perhaps the most painful situation occurs when a biological parent develops apathy for parenting.

were able to help, by being empathic. The father worked with his new mate to understand that his coparent was deeply hurt in childhood, and that she suffered severe and lasting problems as a result. Together, without including graphic details, coparent and stepparent were able to give the boy a supportive understanding of his mother's problems, rather than assign her the hurtful label of "deadbeat." Their empathy toward the boy's mother is passed on to the son, who will be able to grow up without hate and distrust.

Empathic Communication

Divorce occurs for many reasons, and struggles with communication weave a common thread throughout most scenarios of separation. Today's experts who write about the effects of divorce on children recommend that parents learn skills of talking and listening as tools for healing the family. Learning to communicate with empathy requires acceptance of a basic premise about *need*. The idea is that what people want is determined by an underlying need, in almost every instance. For each of us, how we view another person's willingness or unwillingness to fill our needs profoundly affects how we deal with them. Further, how willing we are to help others fill their needs determines our success in relationships.

One key to productive communication lies in deciding whether a conversation is for our own need fulfillment or for another person's sake, and then talking and listening accordingly. A father who needs help from his coparent in getting the kids to or from activities may decide to bring up the topic with his former wife. Or a stepmother who notices that her crossparent

The idea is that what people want is determined by an underlying need.

seems angry may try to help the children's mother with her feelings. In either case, the decision as to whose need will be addressed guides the rest of the conversation.

The Triangle of Decision

Interpersonal problems take considerable thought to resolve well, whether the discomfort is primarily our own or whether the issue belongs to someone else. Whenever signals of trouble are set off, it will help to take time to decide what **to** do. When a statement or comment by your coparent or crossparent triggers an emotional flare-up, tell yourself to stop, think, and decide what to say or do next.

A basic three-point paradigm tells you how to decide. When you notice there is a problem:

- Decide to help or get help
- Give help with reflective listening
- Get help with the polite request

The paradigm can easily be diagrammed:

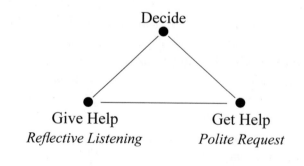

Decide

Give Help
Reflective Listening

Get Help
Polite Request

Decide to Help or Get Help

The first step in addressing problem resolution is to figure out who has the issue before you take a stance. If the problem belongs to your coparent or your child you will proceed to the skill of *reflective listening* so you can help him or her find a solution. If the problem is your own, though, you will activate the *polite request* to help yourself get what you want.

Deciding who has the problem may take a little work. Consider the examples below to see how you might find out.

Your child's other parent needs a sense of success in parenting.

Example 1

Your Coparent:	*We have to have a talk.*
You:	*What's the matter now?*
Your Coparent:	*Our son is failing in school.*
You:	*Well, maybe he should suffer the consequences.*
Your Coparent:	*I couldn't live with that.*
You:	*Okay, let's talk a little more.*

Here your coparent has the problem, and you will choose the skill of *reflective listening*. It may have seemed at first that your failing son owns the problem, or it may feel like your coparent is blaming you and making it your problem. But the real issue is your coparent's feelings about failure. Your child's other parent needs a sense of success in parenting, and validating that will help you both find a way to deal with your son.

Example 2

You:	*I'm thinking of moving out of town with our daughter.*
Your Coparent:	*You're not allowed to do that!*

> You: *I don't have any choice. I've just been laid off at work.*
> Your Coparent: *So what do you want me to do about it?*
> You: *You're going to have to let me move.*
> Your Coparent: *I certainly am not!*

Here you notice that you are feeling emotional, but this time the problem is your own. So far your coparent is not motivated to help you or empathize with your plight. This situation calls for the skill of making a *polite request* to get your coparent to understand. Continuing the sequence of blocked communication will only be frustrating to both of you. After studying how to listen to others below, read about how to ask for help yourself by making a polite request.

Give Help with Reflective Listening

Chapter 1 introduced *reflective listening* as a way of helping your children cope with their feelings about separation. Now we apply this valuable skill to situations where stepparents or coparents need your help. Letting another adult know you understand what they are feeling will lead you to the quickest resolution of the problem.

> Child's Stepmother: *The kids have been acting like monsters.*
> You: *You seem to be pretty irritated with them.*
> Child's Stepmother: *I'm about at the end of my rope.*
> You: *I imagine you're quite frustrated.*
> Child's Stepmother: *I am! I'm not used to so much noise and commotion all day.*

You: *I think I know what you're going*
through. They can be a handful.
Child's Stepmother: *Thanks for understanding.*

In this instance a defensive retort such as "Don't you dare call my children monsters" would have led to conflict and hard feelings all around. Sometimes hanging in with compassion and patient reflection is the best way you can respond.

Get Help with the Polite Request

This simple skill, which was presented in Chapter 3, has been emphasized by psychologist P. Leslie Herold as an important strategy for parents to use across households. Built on the traditional concept of the *I message*, the *polite request* is structured to stimulate empathy in a listener by having the speaker talk about his or her own feelings before asking the listener for help. The idea is that when we express our feelings about what is happening, the listener is more likely to hear us and care.

Sample "I Messages"

- *I feel angry when our daughter says she has no clean clothes at your house.*

- *I worry when our son stays out past dark.*

In situations of divorce and remarriage, this way of stating your own emotions works better than a hostile "You Message."

- *You don't wash our daughter's clothes.*

- *You let our son stay out too late.*

Dr. Herold uses the I message to construct a format for expressing our needs or wants in a carefully worded way.

Format of the Request

Let's use the example of the parent who wants to move to another town to illustrate how the polite request should work.

First, state what happened:
> *I've just been laid off at work.*

Second, state your feeling:
> *I'm worried about being able to support our daughter.*

Third, explain the basis of your feeling:
> *I've looked for other jobs here ~ there isn't anything available and I have to find work soon.*

Fourth, state your request:
> *I'd like to move to a town about thirty miles from here where I have located a good position.*

Fifth, say what you will do in return:
> *If you will agree to consider the move, I will work with you on re-arranging the schedule so our daughter doesn't miss any of her time with you.*

Sixth, ask if your request can be granted:
> *Do you think you can work with me on this?*

Even though your coparent may not be able to grant your immediate request, asking for what you need in a polite way will stimulate a productive talk. Effective problem-solving always begins with identification of the issue and discussion about why the problem should be solved. The polite request works because it gives you a way to present your dilemma in a form that elicits empathy.

Interactive Listening

Encouraging another parent to "fill your need" without making a demand is an important strategy for getting along. Equally important, though, is the art of listening when your coparent or crossparent has a need. When the *polite request* and *reflective listening* are used in the same conversation, an *interactive listening* dialogue takes place. Former spouses or other parents take turns expressing how they feel and asking for what they need. Each responds to the other in ways that clarify the problem and with ideas or suggestions that help.

Study this conversation to see where empathy comes in.

I hate the new day care center we picked!

Wow! You are really mad!

Of course I am! I'm angry!

Can you tell me what is wrong?

When I arrive to pick up the kids and see that there's no adult on duty, I start to worry about safety! I'd like to find a place with better supervision.

Oh. I can understand that you get upset when you see the children unattended. I would feel the same way myself.

I'd like to ask you to help me look for a better center. Would that be all right with you?

Yes.

The power of empathic communication is enormous. With it, we can get more of what we need from others, and give them more of what they need. Without empathy we are likely

When the polite request and reflective listening are used in the same conversation, an interactive listening dialogue takes place.

to remain in a void of interpersonal doubt, feeling misunderstood, and misunderstanding others.

How Empathy Heals

The point of this chapter has been to illustrate how compassionate understanding can make parenting after divorce go more smoothly. The way separated and recoupled spouses choose to talk and listen to each other in large part determines the measure of their success. Even if one or two parents in the family battery can develop empathy for the others, the entire unit will benefit.

Empathy provides another advantage to families that has to do with healing. Every time angry interactions are replaced by more pleasant, caring dialogues, hurting former spouses feel a little better about themselves, and also about each other. When old habits are broken and replaced with better ones, painful emotions like guilt and remorse are replaced with feelings of hope, and a sense of optimism is restored. While life must always go on as families try to recoup from their losses, the road to repair is smoothest when empathic rebuilding is a focus.

Even when sympathy and sensitivity are in the mix as well as understanding, the task of getting past grief after divorce and remarriage is a life-long process of healing. Hundreds of factors affect the course of recovery for every separated mother and father, but the wounds of those treated with empathy will be fixed the fastest. Try to remember that the biggest key to your own well-being may lie in the help you offer to your child's parents in the other home.

Chapter 6

RULEBOOK FOR THE FAMILY OF PARENTS

Reasons for Rules in Families

A family is formed when a man and woman decide to live together, with or without a marriage. Children are brought in by natural birth, by adoption, or in the case of stepfamilies, by remarriage. Whenever groups of people coexist in a defined space, rules naturally develop to provide structure, reduce confusion, and create order. Family members grow to know how to behave and interact with each other in the interest of getting along.

The divorce boom that started in the 1960s is now several decades old, and although the divorce rate is finally dropping, it is still alarmingly high. Over the past twenty years, standards have evolved for mothers and fathers raising children while living apart. Now there is a virtual code of conduct for separated and divorced families. Though no longer living under one roof, divorced families are still families, with mothers, fathers, and children living in two homes. More than ever, separated families need rules, such as those outlined in parenting plans, to keep the peace.

Standards for successful stepparenting, such as those alluded to in the stepfamily parenting plan at the end of Chapter 4, are less refined than those for divorced coparents, but they are now a modern reality too. Some 70 percent of all children eventually spend time in a stepfamily, and guidelines have emerged to prevent chaos in second-order families. Without blood relations between all members, and without each parent having a primary bond with each child, stepfamilies need rules even more than divorced families.

Expectations are now beginning to evolve for parents in the configuration I call crossparents – the same-sex parents in different homes. Second spouses who assume a role in the lives of stepchildren have no real bond to the child's other parent, and stepparents will always have weaker ties to the children. These honorary parents still play important roles in the daily functioning of the family, though, especially after legal remarriage and after the first two years. Over time, stepparents come to provide substantial extended support for their spouses' children as well as hands-on help with caretaking.

A Triad of Golden Rules

Three general rules are fundamental to the well-being of children in separated, divorced, and remarried families.

Golden Rule #1. Put the Needs of the Children First

This rule is the premise of this book. Decisions can be hard to make in times of family transition, but one decision every loving father and mother should make is to consider the needs of their children ahead of their own. More easily said than done, this guideline requires ongoing concessions and sacrifices by the parents. Too often, though, stress leads directly to triangulation between family members, with boys and girls getting caught in the middle.

Parents and stepparents following the rule of *children first* understand that boys and girls love both their natural parents and that they always will. They respect the child's right to be taken care of thoughtfully, to be listened to, and to be loved. They make efforts to let children be children and refrain from drawing them into conflict.

Putting children first means controlling destructive emotions at difficult moments, making extra efforts to be certain youngsters feel important in both homes, and keeping the children emotionally safe. Since girls and boys choose neither marriage nor divorce, they have the right to expect parents to arrange things for them in peaceful, loving ways.

Golden Rule #2. Respect the Parenting Chain of Command

An overlay of confusion can make parents uncertain as to their roles in the family constellation, and this rule requires elaboration. In original families the parents are in charge. Mothers and fathers together provide discipline and structure as to what the children can and cannot do, and help the children solve problems. Even when one parent tends to dominate, the children look to both parents to fill their primary needs.

Most parents who conclude that a child will be better off with their new partner are making a serious error.

Whenever a family divorces, the parents – now coparents living apart – are still in charge of their children. Parenting from different homes, effective coparents talk and discuss things before deciding what is in their child's best interest. Even when parents have trouble ending their personal relationship and even when conflict is high, fathers and mothers should try to parent as a team.

As time goes by after divorce, most families evolve into another form of family, which includes other adults. Significant others, fiancées, and stepparents enter the child's world, and this stage of family development becomes critical. New partners do not replace parents, nor do they assume equal say in the chain of command. Each child's divorced coparents remain at the head of his or her own family unit, while other adults become consultants in the parenting domain.

Dynamics of loss and grief can make acceptance of the chain of command difficult for both a coparent and the new chosen partner. "How am I to do this?" you might say, feeling you have a right to move on with someone else in your life. "This new person will be perfect for my children," you might think, perhaps believing that your new partner will be a better parent than the other parent ever was.

Most parents who conclude that a child will be better off with their new partner are making a serious error. Your children still mourn the loss of your intact family and will become sad and confused when their allegiance to either natural parent is threatened. When coparents and stepparents fight over rights to status in the parenting coalition, they are destined to have unhappy homes.

Golden Rule #3. Use Your Family Manners

The language parents and stepparents use in communicating about the children, and the manner in which they speak to each other, affect the quality of parenting the children receive after their mothers and fathers remarry. As pointed out earlier, many of the basic niceties we learned early in life are of utmost importance in building sound working relationships in two homes.

Parenting partners determined to follow this important rule should review Chapter 5, which details ways to communicate successfully. Using a polite style of interaction will control conflict between households and lead to better problem solving. Most importantly, when parents use manners while working out problems, they model peace and patience for their children, giving them skills they can use for a lifetime.

The Emotional Price of Breaking Rules

Most rules in the domain of human relationships are, by their nature, just guidelines for success in interactions with others. Only in the most extreme or abusive instances will a court of law intervene when mothers or fathers make mistakes in their parenting. Far more often, there are no concrete penalties to pay when children suffer the consequences of their parents' unintentional or purposeful errors.

Children are not scarred forever by divorce unless their mothers and fathers fail to put their children's needs first. Over and over, we see that boys and girls who grow up amidst high parental conflict are those most at risk for a troubled adulthood. Remarriage takes place because of a parent's attempt to rebuild well-being and happiness, but where a second marriage fails, children are even worse off. Youngsters who endure years of tension try to create equilibrium by balancing the family themselves, and subsequently forego their own development.

Let it suffice to say that parents who truly love their children will voluntarily follow guidelines for successful parenting after divorce and remarriage. Where education is necessary they will seek guidance from professionals and open their minds to new ideas. Since there is no end to the responsibility of a parent, at least until a child is grown, parents who falter should try hard and try again. And where specific rules have not been developed because of changes in societal norms, the triad of golden rules should still apply.

~~~~~~~~~~~~~~~~~~~

The Coparenting Code of Conduct

This document is presented as a summary of model standards for all parents living apart, divorced, separated, or never having been married. To get the most out of it, use it as a checklist. Rate yourself on each behavior listed under the ten standards in the checkboxes. Give yourself three points where you see yourself as doing a good job, two where you are doing a fair job, and one or zero where you are doing poorly. Then add up the points. Parents who score 75-90 are coparenting well. Scores of 60-75 reflect fair coparenting, and scores below 60 reveal poor coparenting performance.

If you or your partner scores low on this checklist, consider helping yourself by reading some of the books listed in the References section at the end of this book.

1. Form a neutral business relationship with the other parent, putting personal and marital issues aside. Eliminate hostility, arguing, and conflict from your coparenting relationship, and settle disagreements at business meetings that concern the children.

☐	Address issues one at a time
☐	Compromise whenever you can
☐	Put issues of the past behind you

2. Maintain communication about your child. Keep each other informed about school and all important aspects of your child's life. Resort to modified parallel parenting when you have conflict, using phone, email, fax, and journals on a regular basis.

☐	Attend school conferences together
☐	Thank each other for helping out with parenting
☐	Include each other in important events

3. Assure children they are not at fault for divorce or separation. Tell each child they are loved by each parent, and avoid explanations that blame either one of you. If you are driven to be "honest" and give your child the "truth," take care in how you proceed.

☐	Seek guidance from a child counselor when you need to
☐	Protect your child from unnecessary, hurtful details
☐	Give age-appropriate explanations

4. Handle the adult business yourselves. Children should not be asked to deliver messages, notes, or money. When problems arise, ask the other parent to talk or meet.

☐	Respond to each other's requests promptly
☐	Keep your children out of the middle
☐	Thank each other for working things out

5. Speak to the child in positive or neutral terms about the other parent. Absolutely never criticize or berate your coparent in front of your child.

☐	Talk to your child about the other parent's strengths
☐	Use empathy to get beyond anger
☐	Keep negative beliefs to yourself

6. Encourage time-sharing with the other parent by showing enthusiasm when taking the child to the other parent. Just "going along with" parenting time schedules is sometimes not enough. When a child resists, talk to the other parent about addressing the child's reactions, and take steps to work things out.

☐	Do not discontinue parenting time when your child complains
☐	Make the child's time with the other parent a priority, even if inconvenient
☐	Get guidance from a specialist when you need to

7. Exercise your own parenting time with flexibility and consistency. Avoid repeatedly canceling or missing your time and stick as close to the regular schedule as you can.

	Make up missed time right away
	Do not "keep score" by counting missed hours or minutes
	Prioritize quality over quantity of time

8. Respect the other parent's time with your child. Schedule activities only with the input of both of you, and limit your phone calls to the other home.

	Honor a child's request to contact the other parent
	Show enthusiasm for your child's activities on the other parent's time
	Call children no more than every other day

9. Allow your child to have privacy in his or her relationship with the other parent. Strive for a balance between showing interest and allowing privacy.

☐	Avoid "grilling" your child for information
☐	Convey approval or neutrality about the other home
☐	When your child is quiet, respect his or her need for space

10. Consider your child's needs before your own. This means recognizing that your children need both parents.

☐	Make sure your child does not miss out on things because of your own feelings of discomfort
☐	When you believe your child needs less time with the other parent, consult with a counselor before you reduce parenting time
☐	Continue your coparenting education by reading or attending specialized classes

Good Parents Consider Needs of the Children First

A Primer for Positive Stepparenting

The practices below are a summary of suggestions for step-mothers and stepfathers joining families with another parent's children. Reflect on how well you are doing with each guide-line as you read through the list, so you can work on making improvements where they are needed.

Practice 1. **Accept the fact that your family will be different from what you expect.** Most stepparents find life with a spouse's children to be very different from what they thought it would be like. So many variables are involved in remarried families that anticipating what things will be like is almost impossible. Be ready to change your views about how your new spouse and the children will get along, and about how the family should function. By remembering the keys of flexibility and balance in forming your family identity, you will have the best chance of being satisfied.

Practice 2. **Form bonds with your stepchildren at a pace they can accept and with a style that will work for them.** The process of bonding involves first being acquaint-ed with your spouse's child before you become a friend, and long before deep caring can develop. Follow the lead of the child in doing things together, and help your stepchild with homework, chores, and problem solving. Be grateful if love develops between you, but don't be disappointed if it doesn't. Stepfamilies characterized by positive regard and mutual respect between parents and children are the happiest.

Practice 3.   **Leave discipline to the child's natural parent after giving input to your spouse.** Children in the process of bonding with a stepparent need to be nurtured by the new adult, and negative interactions will prevent a strong union from developing. Stepparents should support their spouses in handling behavioral issues, and together both parents in the home should decide about consequences. Telling the child about restrictions or loss of privileges, however, should be handled by the original parent when possible. Children have developed lifelong bonds with the natural parent which help buffer the blows of discipline, and the unconditional love they feel keeps resentment in check.

Practice 4.   **Talk to your spouse about the children in private, and in organized meetings when possible.** The forum for discussions about the children is the spousal business meeting. A child who overhears stressful conversations about his or her behavior, or about the other parent, can be hurt by what is said. Arguing in front of children and stepchildren will weaken their sense of family unity. After you have discussed issues together in private, organize a household family meeting to talk to the children.

Practice 5.   **Give your family time to grow, but always make efforts to move on.** Building a healthy stepfamily takes time. Weeks, months, and even years may go by before a sense of "normalcy" is developed. Try to accept this fact and be patient while you continue to work on relationships. This means that even if a stepchild is in serious conflict with you, you keep trying to strengthen the tie.

Practice 6. **Recognize problems as they confront you, but avoid competition in solving them.** Denial is a defense mechanism early in stepfamily life which should wane within the first twelve months. Be on guard for problems that can develop in your relationship with your spouse, in your efforts to bond with your stepchild, or in your crossparent relationship, and talk with your spouse about addressing them. Avoid trying to outdo the child's parent in the other home or competing for a child's affection.

Practice 7. **Defer to the child's natural parents when behavioral problems are happening in both homes.** Revert to your role as supporter of your spouse when stress between the coparents is high. Remember to step back from confrontation, and to step up to productive problem solving.

Practice 8. **Keep expectations in check. Realize that love from a stepchild cannot be legislated, and that it may never develop.** Most children will always have unconditional love for their biological parents; love for the stepparent, if it comes, will be secondary. Try to be content with less and aim for a respectful friendship with your stepchild.

Practice 9. **Strive for balance in your marriage and in your family.** Remember the importance of flexibility in getting what you want from your spouse, from your children, and from your stepchildren. Set realistic personal goals and enjoy small moments of gratification. Try to focus on what you have rather than on what is missing from your relationships and your life.

Practice *10.*   **Emphasize your loving marital relationship and make it your destination for when the children are grown.** Remember that your marriage will long outlast the years you and your spouse will be raising the children. When they are grown and living on their own, you will still be their parents, but your involvement will change dramatically. Prepare for the future by building a strong and resilient bond with your spouse.

Crossparenting Fundamentals

Crossparenting is the most recent parental role to become a focus of attention by counselors who work with families after remarriage. Guidelines are now emerging for same-sex parents in each home to follow. These suggestions are offered for families with mother-stepmother or father-stepfather parenting dyads.

For Stepparent as a Crossparent

1.   Remember to acknowledge the child's same-sex biological parent in the other household, at least with basic respect. When you encounter your spouse's former partner, make eye contact, smile, and say hello. Extend the same courtesy to the child's other stepparent from the other home, if there is one. Though you may have good reason to harbor negative feelings, even about both adults in the other home, it will help to keep those feelings to yourself.

> **Example:** *You are a stepmother. At your stepson's baseball game, the boy's mother arrives late and must walk in front of you to take the only seat left in the bleachers. Seeing her sets off many feelings, and you think the easiest way to cope*

is by ignoring her. In the best interest of bonding with your stepson, though, you acknowledge your crossparent and say good morning. The boy then smiles at both of you, pleased that his mom and stepmom seem to be getting along.

2. Defer to the biological parent whenever you can, especially when the mom or dad is very involved with the children. Divorced coparents who live close to each other can conveniently raise their children while living apart. By marrying into the family you have taken on a supporting role, and there will be many times when you should opt out of parenting tasks, especially when they are optional.

Example: *You are a stepfather. It's the first day of school for your second-grade stepdaughter. This is your new wife's parenting day, but she has been called in to her office early. While dropping the girl off at school you see that her father has come to wish her well, and to meet the second grade teacher. You would love to go to the class-room yourself, but you politely defer to your crossparent, say goodbye to your stepchild, and leave.*

For Parent as a Crossparent

1. Accept the fact that your child now has another parent in the coalition of caretakers. You may think that your former spouse has remarried too soon, or you may not get along with the new spouse. You may feel anxious about the parenting style of this newcomer to the family, or you may feel you are be-ing replaced. Once remarriage has taken place, however, your children have a stepparent, and this is your new reality. It will help to use self-talk at this point, and reassure yourself of your

primary importance to your son or daughter. You will never be replaced, but your child's family of parents has grown.

Example: *You are the mother of two children. While shopping at the mall with the kids, you have a chance encounter with your crossparent. You make eye contact with her in the aisle, and have a choice about how you react. The children seem excited about running into their new stepmother, though, and you choose to have a brief talk. After you chat and then go on with your shopping, the children chime, "That was fun!" No matter how you felt at the moment, you handled the situation well, and the kids are better off because of it.*

2. Defer to the stepparent when you can, especially during your coparent's scheduled time with the children. Remember that this new spouse is helping your child's other parent with the caretaking, and this is a benefit to you all. It may help to acknowledge that the commitment of marriage gives a stepparent a recognized role. By stepping back, you do a service to your child, who will happily accept a second parent of your sex if you will.

Example: *You are the father of a school-aged girl. Your daughter has a difficult project to complete for math class. You know you could easily help her, but her step-dad teaches math at the college level, and your child will be in the other home most of the week. Your crossparent offers to take the lead in helping her, and you respectfully defer to him in this instance. Your daughter successfully finishes the project, and both you and her stepfather are proud of her.*

Ten Tips for the Network of Parents

I offer these ideas for families where there are two homes and three or four parents involved.

1. Divorced coparents should make major decisions regarding their children together. If the *parenting plan* delegates major decision-making to just one parent, the other parent should still be consulted for input. For example, if a mother is the appointed decision-maker for choices about school, she should remember to consult with the father before choosing the school for the child. Your children do best when they know *both* original parents have had a hand in making important arrangements for them.

2. When the services of a professional are needed, such as mediation for divorced parents, the stepparents or significant others usually do not attend. Especially in the first stage of stepfamily life, which is usually the first two years, stepmoms and stepdads should respect the coparents' need to work together without the direct presence of third and fourth parties. The children need to see their original parents working together as a team before the entire league becomes involved. Also, the stepparents do not have an equal *say* in major decisions for their partner's children, at least until sometime later. Groups of three or four parents in a family should consider joint meetings only when there is a real basis of trust all around.

3. Stepparents have direct say about household rules in the home in which they are living. Coparent and stepparent should have *spousal meetings* to talk about what they expect and need. If both partners have children, they may decide that slightly different rules apply to the two sets of girls and boys in the interest of putting the needs of each child first. Alternatively they may decide on a single set of rules, getting input from all the children at household *family meetings*. These decisions about in-home expectations are considered to be minor everyday decisions, and there is no specific reason for parents in the other home to be consulted. To achieve consistency where possible, however, a thoughtful divorced coparent might check with the parent in the other home about rules such as bedtimes, chores, and curfews.

4. Crossparents do not usually have close working relationships with each other, especially in the first two years. Every divorced coparent needs time to adjust to a former spouse being with someone else, and children need time to experience their *parents* working together before they observe a stepparent getting close to their other parent. When the children's coparents have achieved a successful business relationship, stepparents can effectively become more directly involved. At this point, a divorced mother may become more friendly with the children's stepparent, or a stepfather may take steps to get to know the children's father better.

5. The terms "mother" and "father" or "mom" and "dad" should usually be reserved for the children's original parents, and stepparents should usually be called by their first names. This simple practice eliminates much confusion for the child, and helps solidify an accurate perception of the family constellation. Stepparents who feel "slighted" because they believe the children want to use the affectionate term for them are urged to be patient and to realize that the second *golden rule* preserves the importance of every boy or girl's biological parent. When either of the natural parents feels adamant that the affectionate term of "mom" or "dad" be reserved only for her or him, the stepparent should accept being on a first-name basis.

6. After the first two years of remarried life, and after the divorced parents are working together well, coparents and stepparents might consider having *combined network meetings* to talk about the children when necessary. These sessions should be held in a neutral place and not in either coparent's home in order to give each set of parents a sense of equal footing. Before peace has been achieved between the two parents who used to be married, however, these joint efforts to include the input of new as well as original parents will fail. Sometimes there are entirely too many variables and personality differences among a set of four parents to expect harmonious results. Indeed, many parents and stepparents who have tried this strategy too soon have reported disastrous results.

7. When there is stress between divorced parents, and when another member of the evolving parenting network is especially adept at communication, this individual may be able to help by serving in the role of an informal *parenting network mediator*. A stepparent or new partner may be a flexible individual for whom achieving balance and making good suggestions comes naturally. In these cases it can be wise to have this helpful family member be the one to talk to the coparent or stepparent in the other home. Sometimes issues can be worked out without structured meetings, or the neutral parent may lead a meeting of all the parents together.

8. In families where months or years have gone by with continuing conflict and hostility between divorced parents, serious steps are needed. Here the natural parents should go back to strengthening their basic business relationship because no other intervention is going to work. They should think about enrolling in comprehensive *coparenting education classes,* which will help them transform their poor relationship into a better one. Stepparents should also take these steps, but because the coparents need to improve their style of relating to each other first, steppartners should usually enroll in separate classes. Whatever steps they take, it is essential that parents and stepparents commit to learning to work together better.

9. After learning about the skills of communication for working together, parents and stepparents may wish to locate a counselor who might agree to become an ongoing *parenting coordinator* for them. Using the services of a professional on a regular basis may at first seem like an extreme step, but families who do so are able to function in peace from day to day because there is an unbiased resource to help them. Check with your local court if you have trouble locating a parenting coordinator.

10. When children in either home develop significant problems, such as depression, worrisome behavior problems, or acting out in the community, even more help is necessary In the most serious instances of family discord you may need therapists for your children and yourselves, as well as parenting coordinators, throughout your stepfamily life. Loving divorced parents and stepparents will not hesitate to provide the help and care the family needs in order to function smoothly. Nothing is worse for children than suffering through years of family conflict, and nothing is better for them than living in peace.

Where Rules Have Not Been Written

I provided these guidelines to help divorced coparents and stepparents organize their parenting efforts. Because of the thousands of variables involved in building families, though, and because personalities are all unique, no parenting guide could address every situation that might arise. Mothers, fathers, and parenting partners are therefore certain to encounter scenarios where they are at a loss about what to do.

The best rule of thumb to apply when confusing circumstances arise is to wait, gather more information, and get advice from a trusted source before you begin to act. The adage "When in Doubt, Don't" can keep you from behaving impulsively in difficult situations when your emotions spur you to act without thinking. Too many parents express regret about how they handled things under pressure of the moment after a crisis between the homes is over.

The *golden rules* of parenting as a coalition should be reviewed and reconsidered every time a new dilemma comes up. These basic tenets should govern in times where no member of the parenting network is certain about how to handle the situation, or where there is disagreement among members of the parenting team. Your children deserve the best parenting they can get from all caretakers in both of their homes.

~~~~~~~~~~~~~~~~

Chapter 7

BENDING, FLEXING AND BUILDING

Fulfilling the Parenting Contract

Men and women who marry enter a formal contract which is sealed with a marriage certificate. When they bring children into the family, though, there is no formal agreement about parenting and no requirement that they learn any rules about caretaking. Instead, mothers and fathers enter *unwritten contracts* to parent their children together, raising sons and daughters to adulthood. When the unfortunate advent of divorce brings an end to the legal contract of marriage, the unwritten agreement to parent the children stays intact. However, it is the written parenting plan in the divorce decree that formalizes the parents' responsibilities.

When parents marry a second time they again have a written contract for the personal union, but only an unwritten contract that involves the children of the stepcouple. This time the agreement is even looser than the informal contract in the first marriage. Again our system seems to assume that all parenting figures will take part in nurturing the children, but stepparents have no legal parenting rights, and the way they will take part is not defined.

Unspoken understandings and assumptions between parents and stepparents are often inadvertently ignored or forgotten at the expense of the children. As I suggested in Chapter 4, parents in second marriages might consider writing out the details of their intentions for parenting the children together. Until this practice becomes more common, though, only unwritten stepfamily parenting plans will guide these new relationships.

Since children are not responsible for either divorce or remarriage, it is their needs, rather than those of any of the parents, that should drive the family system.

In this chapter I address how parents and stepparents can follow the first *Golden Rule*, Put the Needs of the Children First, to use an adaptive approach to parenting without detailed and written plans. Since children are not responsible for either divorce or remarriage, it is *their* needs, rather than those of any of the parents, that should drive the family system. Again the contract may be unwritten, but parents who follow this guiding rule and at least talk about how they intend to parent together will have the happiest families.

Working on the Coparenting Relationship
One theme of this book has been that the first step in organizing your efforts on behalf of children after remarriage is to focus on your relationship with your former partner or spouse. Grief often prompts hurting women or men to move ahead too quickly, finding new significant others who can help them through the storm of divorce. The best thing you can do for your boys or girls, though, is to take the time and effort required to transform your pre-divorce relationship with your

child's other parent into a healthy post-divorce relationship. In review, the stages of development in the coparenting relationship as they progress toward healing are:

Stage 1. Conflictual, with many disagreements, rigidity over parenting issues, and poor communication.

Stage 2. Disengaged, with fewer disagreements but with little communication and a split life style for the child.

Stage 3. Cooperative, with flexibility in problem solving, productive communication, and an integrated life for the child.

Parents who recouple while their coparenting relationship is still in Stage 1 are destined to have problems no matter how much time has passed since the divorce. Those who have progressed to Stage 2 may experience less stress from the other household, but the children's lives will be divided and not completely gratifying. Only coparents who have managed to become cooperative and to carry on with mutual respect can expect their girls and boys to thrive. The reason, put simply, is that their needs have become their parents' primary focus, and the rule of *what is best for the children* has been carried forward into second marriages.

If you are a parent who has gone on to remarry while your coparenting relationship with your former partner is still poor, you have two simultaneous tasks. For the sake of your children you will need to work at improving your coparenting relationship at the same time you work at building bonds in your new stepfamily. The emotional health of your children is at stake, and many kinds of change will be required of you. Keep this fact in mind as you read about specific problems later in this chapter.

Working on Stepfamily Growth

A well-known saying is that the only thing certain in life is change, and surely this is true in second families. For each stepfamily the experience of blending is different, and as time goes by each new family develops individuality with varying degrees of conflict, harmony, and the ability to work through problems. In Chapter 2 I pointed out that the first two years of remarriage are always difficult, that the middle years can be smooth, and that later years in stepfamily life can become rough again, as adolescents pull away from their parents and begin the process of leaving home.

The next sections address common problems that emerge in combined families and list ideas for dealing with them. In addition to recognizing that the status of your coparenting relationship with your former partner is crucial, another key is recognizing which stage of development your new family is in, and being sensitive to stages in child development as well. Creating a family with very young children at the time of remarriage is worlds apart from creating one with teenagers. Infants and school age children are easier to manage and have many years ahead to form bonds with stepparents, but adolescents may cling to the family of origin, forever refusing to merge.

First it will help to review three of the most important features of healthy stepfamilies. The happiest second-time families are those in which:

Each new family develops individuality with varying degrees of conflict, harmony, and the ability to work through problems.

1. New spouses work hard to form a strong and loving marital unit.

2. Both spouses learn to effectively coparent with adults in the other home.

3. Stepparents succeed at building positive bonds with the children.

Setting these qualities as goals will guide coparents and stepparents in the direction of well-being for the family. None of them should take priority over the others, but all three should remain important as the years go by. Remember that balance is always a goal, and in most situations there is more than one way to achieve it.

Discipline in Stepfamilies

Perhaps no issue brings divorced coparents to blows more often than the matter of discipline in a stepfamily. Counselors who work with families are all too familiar with the objections a mother or father raises when a stepparent in the other home handles the children in a punitive or abusive way. Leaving stepparents entirely out of the discipline arena is also unacceptable, however, as it is unrealistic to expect new spouses to have no say over what goes on in their home.

Problems created over discipline can affect all members of the family. A child sent to her room by a stepparent may resent the new caretaker and refuse to develop a relationship. A parent who observes his new spouse stepping in too vigorously when a child misbehaves may become overprotective and edge the

Perhaps no issue brings divorced coparents to blows more often than the matter of discipline in a stepfamily.

stepparent out. A teenager deprived of privileges by a stepparent may shift loyalty to the other home, and a sympathetic coparent receiving the child may unwittingly alienate the child from the other home.

Who Will Discipline the Children?

Discussions about discipline often get stonewalled because of a misunderstanding about the purpose of discipline. In reality, discipline is training about life for children, and we expect this training to produce patterns of appropriate social behavior. Parents teach children about the concepts of right and wrong by the ways they coach their boys and girls about their actions, and by what they do after certain behaviors occur. Often confused with the word punishment, discipline is really a larger concept that has both positive and negative aspects.

Experts find that stepparents get into trouble when they punish their spouse's children.

To me, punishment includes spanking and other physical responses to misbehavior, as well as verbal scolding and lecturing. Experts find that stepparents get into trouble when they punish their spouse's children. The problems that result are twofold. First, punishment is negative discipline that triggers anger and resentment in the child, and it interferes with the bonding process. When an adult who is still new in the child's life inflicts pain physically or verbally, the child will naturally pull away and become wary of the adult. Biological parents can sometimes punish their children without creating resentment because the child has a lifelong base of love to soften the pain. Stepparents do not have such a base of love and trust, however, and can instill fear by punishing a stepchild.

The second problem that results when a stepparent punishes a stepchild is related to the process of grief. The child's parent in the other home, often still feeling guilty and inadequate because of the divorce, can feel helpless about protecting his or her child from the pain of punishment, and may lash out in anger as a result. Statements such as "Don't you dare touch my child again," often follow an incident of physical discipline, and in the worst cases police and authorities become involved. The simple fact is that ugly situations often develop between parents in the two homes when stepparents step in to punish.

Read the following material about how stepparents can participate in disciplining children without inflicting punishment.

The Forum of the Spousal Meeting

One formula that works is for parent and stepparent to sit down and talk about the matter of discipline in their home, discussing household rules and expectations for each spouse's children. Decisions are made at these meetings about which behaviors will be acceptable and which will not be tolerated. Next, these decisions are made clear to the children so they know what to expect. Then, when misbehaviors occur, the stepparent does not punish the child or deliver the consequence directly. Instead, the biological parent tells the child about the punishment or consequence that both parents have chosen. Consequences such as losing privileges are more effective than physical punishment, even when delivered by the biological parent. Though it can take considerable time to talk through each partner's feelings about behavioral standards beforehand and to decide which privileges will be lost, coming to terms with what you will do can resolve the matter of discipline.

In stepfamilies where both spouses have children, three kinds of rules might result from *spousal meetings*:

1. **Household rules that apply to all the children.**
Examples that might apply across the board include
mealtimes, limits on children entering each other's
bedrooms, and rules for respecting each other's
property. Spouses who need ideas about setting up
the household rules may decide to check with the
children themselves for their thoughts. Separate
family meetings as proposed in earlier chapters may
be invaluable as part of this process for getting input
from the children.

2. **Home-to-home rules that apply to only one set of
natural brothers and sisters.** One example of this
type of rule comes about when divorced coparents
in separate homes decide at a business meeting that
their children need different bedtimes from their
stepsisters and stepbrothers. Then the remarried
parent who first attended a coparent business meeting may bring a coparenting decision like this one
to the stepfamily *spousal meeting,* where these differences are discussed and decided upon.

3. **Home-to-home rules that apply to both sets of
children.** Curfew limits or spending allowances
might fall into this category, especially when the parents in both homes have developed similar ways of
looking at things and when they work together well.
Separate sets of divorced coparents might still meet
to talk about rules for their own children, but the
parents all may confer on these issues. Spouses in
both homes will give their input to each other in
spousal meetings as well, and these four-way family
rules may govern all the children.

Spousal meetings about discipline are important for deciding what the rules will be in the stepfamily; parent and stepparent should also decide what will happen when one of these rules is broken. Input from parents in the other home should be sought when consistency is important. Most consequences for breaking rules should involve loss of special privileges, and the natural parent should deliver the consequence.

When a delay is necessary because the biological parent is not home when bad behavior occurs, I suggest telling the child that the incident will be discussed by parent and stepparent as soon as they can get together to talk, and that the natural parent will let the child know what will happen. Getting back to a child about a disciplinary consequence should never be put off because he or she is transitioning to the other household for parenting time. Children forced to worry about being in trouble when they come back to either home can become anxious and afraid of their parents.

About Authoritative Parenting

Discipline that involves strict, inflexible rules which seem arbitrary to the children is often described as *authoritarian*, because it is punitive and harsh. Authoritarian discipline is mostly negative, involving verbal criticism, isolation, and physical punishment. This style of handling children almost always fails in stepfamilies, where tolerance and flexibility are basic requirements for success. Many second families even disband within the first two years because a parent or stepparent resorts to using unreasonable power and control with the children.

At the opposite pole is stepfamily parenting with a loose, *permissive* quality that has too few rules and consequences. Here control is virtually handed to the children themselves

Authoritarian discipline almost always fails in stepfamilies, where tolerance and flexibility are basic requirements for success.

because the parents are unable to manage their behavior. This style of discipline might be more positive because there is little discomfort inflicted, but chaos can also be created by the lack of training about self-control. Poor behavior can even be rewarded and reinforced in these families, as parents and step-parents uncertain about their roles let the children do whatever they want to do.

Between the two extremes is *authoritative* parenting, which is firm and also flexible. This kind of discipline takes more time and thought than the other styles, but it results in happier family life. Parent and stepparent are the organizers of rules and expectations of the children, but they consult with their sons and daughters, change rules when requests are reasonable, and explain why consequences occur. Privileges such as television, computer time, or outings with friends are lost when they logically should be, but they are restored when behavior changes for the better. Most important, positive behavior and compliance are rewarded with praise and encouragement.

Physical punishment should rarely be considered as appropriate for either parenting figure to use in a second family, because of its highly negative effect. An exception may occur, however, when a child endangers himself or someone else. A swift slap on the fanny may be delivered to draw attention to the seriousness of safety, for example when a toddler runs out into traffic. A child having a tantrum may need to be held until the episode subsides, or an adolescent about to attack a sibling may need to be physically restrained.

Even when parents are well-versed in authoritative parenting, children sometimes become belligerent, rude, or oppositional with a stepparent, and immediate intervention is needed.

Positive behavior and compliance are rewarded with praise and encouragement.

These instances present the most difficult challenges because stress can trigger the impulse to act without thinking about the best course of action. Here it is important to use self-control, avoid lashing out in anger, and consider options to physical intervention.

When your stepchild has seriously crossed the line, call a *time-out* from the situation and tell the child you will think about how to handle the incident. Then get together with your spouse to decide what should happen next. Last, meet together with the child and have the biological parent talk about what privilege will be lost as a consequence. By presenting a united front while the natural parent delivers the discipline, you will avoid creating resentment in your stepchild.

Discipline with Respect
In addition to deciding who will discipline the children and what techniques will be used, another critical factor is how consequences are delivered. Parents and stepparents frequently claim that the most important thing to them is that children show respect. A repeating theme of this book, however, is that parenting partners also show respect for the children and each other. Here we emphasize the importance of treating boys and girls with esteem when they have misbehaved, and even when they have been disrespectful to their parents.

To avoid falling into harsh or abusive patterns when disciplining children in second families, coparents and their spouses should again reflect on the power of empathy. When children are oppositional, defiant, or hostile, try imagining what they have gone through with regard to their parents' divorce. This practice can help parenting figures learn to enforce rules with concern instead of anger. And thinking about how a child would feel to be slapped, dragged, or pushed should stop any parent, especially a stepparent, from using physical punishment.

Other than in dangerous situations such as those where children need protection from environmental harm, I see physical intervention as disrespectful. This is because physical punishment insults a child's most precious possession, the human body. Parents and stepparents who love their children will work at finding ways to enforce limits and deliver messages of guidance which preserve the child's self-respect.

Other Common Problems

There are a myriad of reasons why problems other than child discipline develop in families after remarriage. All members of the family have needs, and parents overwhelmed with everyday life can have trouble filling those needs. Spouses who divorced the first time because of wounds from early childhood bring those same wounds to a second marriage, and may struggle emotionally again. Patterns often repeat and when additional issues develop as well, parents and children alike become frustrated and disappointed.

Counselors who work with divorced and remarried parents have found it helpful to recommend certain courses of action for common situations. Notice how the qualities of flexibility and balance guide the advice for problems addressed in the sections below.

How to Choose Your Battles
As soon as two families unite under one roof, lifestyle differences become apparent and stress often emerges right away.

The first years of remarried life are bound to be a challenge, as problems about small issues and larger ones arise. The ideas below might help you distinguish smaller issues from those that truly matter, and lead you toward swifter problem resolution.

When a spouse, child, or stepchild raises a concern about a small issue that "doesn't really matter" to you, solve the problem by giving in and being flexible. When the issue does "really matter," though, have a coparent, spousal or family meeting, and then decide what to do.

Examples of very small issues

◆ If your stepdaughter wants dinner at five o'clock so she can go out to visit a friend, accommodate this small request if you can, even if you are accustomed to eating later. The concession will mean a lot to your stepdaughter, and it will strengthen the bond between you.

◆ If your coparent asks you to switch a parenting weekend because a relative is coming to town, try to make it happen, even if you have plans. Granting a reasonable request will pay off in the future when you need a favor returned.

Examples of larger issues

◆ If your son asks to call your new husband "Daddy" and you think this may cause a problem with his father, first call for a coparent meeting. Then follow up with a spousal meeting, and after doing some problem-solving, talk to the child about the solution the parents feel is best. The term a child uses to address a stepparent is often a very important issue that requires careful thought. There are times when a child should be told *not* to address a stepparent with the term reserved for the natural parent, and this is an important matter.

◆ If your new spouse becomes seriously ill and needs some time without your children in the home, talk to your coparent about the problem and ask for more help with parenting. Take the time to explain your situation in a coparent business meeting, and talk to your children about why they will be spending extra time with their other parent. Responding to your new partner with compassion will demonstrate your level of commitment to him or her and show your coparent your level of trust.

In order to avoid forcing your new family to fit a preconceived mold, be ready to respond to matters of importance with time and attention, and always be ready to adapt. Learn to avoid making mountains out of molehills so you can ease through smaller issues and save your energy for resolving larger problems with your soundest judgement.

Living Together Without Remarriage
The first parent to find a new partner after divorce often comes under fire from the other parent. Statistics tell us that 70 percent of parents will remarry within five years of the legal separation. When a former spouse becomes intimate with someone else, though, resistance is often triggered in the parent who is still alone. A divorced wife or husband who moves in with a new partner without an engagement or wedding can expect criticism and claims of immorality. The practice of cohabitation

without marriage may be acceptable in one parent's eyes but entirely wrong in another's, and where children are involved there can be very strong opinions.

Suggestions

- Try to put off living with your new partner for at least a year after your divorce, and for six months after you have begun to date seriously. The **"six month rule"** defined in Chapter 2 applies not only to bringing new adults into your children's lives, but also to moving in with a new partner. Your child needs time to get to know the new adult before he or she comes into the home, and your former spouse needs time to adjust to the reality that you are now with another partner.

- Keep in mind that living together implies intimacy to your children as well as to your former spouse even when you are careful not to display sexuality in your home. Remember also that second marriages are better for children than long live-in situations. The labels "girlfriend" and "boyfriend" are harder for children to accept than the terms "stepmother" and "stepfather," and they imply impermanence to the children.

- If you are thinking about moving in together but have no plans to marry, and if your divorced co-parent is adamant that you keep living separately, take his or her wishes seriously, and don't move in together yet. Parental conflict is the strongest predictor of problems for your children, and you may be able to avoid it by waiting.

Try to put off living with your new partner for at least a year after your divorce, and for six months after you have begun to date seriously.

- If you are already living together and choose not to marry because one or both of you need more time to decide about the depth of your commitment to each other, talk to your children about your intentions, and talk to your child's other parent. Remember to use skills of effective communication as you try to find a workable resolution to this difficult issue.

- Always communicate your personal plans to your child's other parent yourself, even if you know your decision will be upsetting. Rule out living with someone secretly, and be open about what you are doing. Mutual respect between coparents is critically important, and separated parents should be honest with each other about their living situations.

Stepparent Rejection and Parental Alienation

Negative feelings between stepparent and stepchild are most common in the early stages of stepfamily development but can emerge anytime stress or conflict arises. When loyalty to the biological parents is especially important, children can respond to even highly motivated new spouses with refusals to build relationships. Perhaps because mother-child relationships are so highly valued in our culture, stepmothers are rejected more frequently than stepfathers. Hence, the unfair label "wicked stepmother" gets attached to well-meaning spouses in second families even when their participation with the child is entirely appropriate.

An even more difficult dynamic occurs when a disgruntled parent actively alienates a child from the other parent or stepparent. Out of grief, jealousy or spite a divorced father or mother puts down the former spouse or new partner to the child, paints an inaccurate picture of his or her character, and tries to exclude the parent from the child's life. This active discouragement is most often rooted in personal hurt and hostility. It is also related to the dynamic of *negative intimacy*, which keeps a grieving parent connected to the former spouse by exaggerating and complaining about their negative qualities.

Suggestions

+ Stepparents are urged not to take a stepchild's rejection seriously and to keep offering gestures of attention. Bear in mind that the process of bonding is different in every case and that some children never express love or affection for the stepparent. Shoot for becoming a respected friend of the child, and build trust by not expecting more than the child can give.

+ If you are a divorced father or mother receiving criticism from your child's other parent, counteract the effect by parenting your child with excellence and by refusing to respond with negative emotions. Counselors find that sometimes it may help to explain reality about your qualities to your child yourself, but it does not help to "straighten out" the matter in anger by telling your child the other parent is "lying." Counter-alienation will confuse and distress your son or daughter and only make matters worse. Keep in mind that over time your children will judge you by the quality of your own interactions with them, and they will see you as the loving parent you are.

Shoot for becoming a respected friend of the child, and build trust by not expecting more than the child can give.

Over time your children will judge you by the quality of your own interactions with them, and they will see you as the loving parent you are.

- ◆ Avoid becoming an alienating parent by focusing on your former spouse's strengths rather than on his or her weaknesses, especially when talking to your children. Parents who are unable to come up with nice things to say about their former partners are almost certain to hurt the children with alienating behaviors. If current conflicts are making it hard for you to remember the other parent's strong points, try thinking about what was attractive about him or her when you first began your relationship, so you can convey something positive to your child.

- ◆ Remember to continue your divorce education by reading and studying about how your disapproval of your child's other parent or stepparent hurts the child you love. Keep in mind that parents exert enormous influence over their children's adjustment by the way they portray the parent or stepparent in the other home.

Child Support and Money

Remarriage after divorce means that one or both spouses have parenting plans that outline how basic financial support of their children should take place. No matter how clearly written, these contracts about money are rarely viewed as adequate by everyone involved, and there are many reasons why. Children are expensive to raise, and while child support is delegated to cover primary costs for their shelter, food, and clothing, a child's actual needs can easily cost double what the court computes.

Even when separated parents agree on the general lifestyle they intend to give their children, disputes often arise over spending for recreation, activites, and other kinds of optional expenses. Parents' jobs change, medical costs and insurance coverage rise, and keeping track of what is owed between divorced parents presents an enormous task. Serious conflicts often arise in families after remarriage when stress over money persists.

Suspicion is the most common and troublesome emotion connected to problems with money after remarriage. Without first-hand knowledge about how money is spent, parents making payments often wonder if the money is being squandered or mismanaged. Struggling coparents often distrust reports of former spouses about their exact income figures and object to their lavish vacations. Mothers and fathers in both homes can worry about whether the dollars they contribute actually go to support the stepparent's children and not their own.

Suggestions

- Work on developing trust in the coparent business relationship so you don't have to worry that your coparent may be taking advantage of you. Ask your former spouse to sit down with you regularly and talk about how money is spent. Without being intrusive, take away as many unknown factors as you can, so you know what you are dealing with.

- Make a plan with your new mate for managing money within your household. Decide together how each of you will meet the financial needs of your own children, and what you can do for each other. To avoid the development of distrust, communicate often about where you stand financially. To work on the marital bond, have at least one joint bank account where you manage your money together.

♦ To control your emotions around issues of money, review the ideas for coping presented throughout this guide, and remember to use *reflective listening* and the *polite request* in conversations with your spouse or with your coparent.

Conflicting Parenting Time Schedules

Combining two family systems with children often means going along with time-sharing patterns in two other homes. One parent's children may be in your home every other weekend while the other's may live with you half-time. Or your spouse's child may not see the other parent at all, while your own child has an active relationship with your coparent. Sometimes families struggle to have time with all the children together, especially when relationships with former spouses are strained, and when requests for time together are not granted.

Perhaps more than in any other arena, flexibility is the key to dealing with multiple parenting plans.

Parents and children alike develop feelings of insecurity and frustration over hectic schedules that do not mesh. Angry episodes of conflict can erupt and disagreements over other minor issues can seem major. Because sharing children between two homes is taxing, the problems it brings should be anticipated so they can be dealt with patiently. Perhaps more than in any other arena, flexibility is the key to dealing with multiple parenting plans without turmoil.

Suggestions

♦ Remember that for each individual child, time with both original parents is most important. Time to bond with stepsiblings and stepparents is also necessary, but building a healthy second family takes years. Especially in the first two years after divorce, each child must have a considerable amount of time with the other coparent to sustain the primary relationship.

♦ Refresh your understanding of the pie-chart of personal needs. Strive for time slots of togetherness in the most important combinations of family members. You won't feel frustrated with a schedule that is not ideal when you know that most of your children's biggest needs, and at least some of your own, are being met.

♦ Be prepared to change your plans when an opportunity comes up that you have wanted, so you can capitalize on every chance for pleasant times. If your spouse's coparent asks you to take the children at an inconvenient time but it also allows you extra whole-family time, seize the opportunity. In the long run, practicing this kind of adaptability will give you many meaningful parenting moments.

Competition Between Stepsiblings

Children in stepfamilies may deny that jealousy is a problem for them. But feelings of envy are often at the root of overt conflicts that develop between girls and boys who become instant siblings on their parents' wedding day. Imagine how it must feel for a boy from a low-to-moderate income family to suddenly have a wealthy brother. Or think about the reaction of a girl who rarely sees her mother when she moves in with a stepmother who sees her own children almost every day. Although parents may discourage comparisons, children size up the "haves" and "have nots" quickly, and they react with anger or jealousy.

Parents who combine their families should be ready to respond to signs of distress in their children by being ready to talk, listen, and problem-solve. A boy who loses his place as youngest in the family when his parent and stepparent decide to have a child together will need extra attention and support in finding a sense of being special in another way. A girl complaining that things are not "fair" anymore because she has to share a bedroom with a stepsister will need help in working through the problem. And all children refusing to accept siblings not biologically related to them will need understanding.

Suggestions

- Watch out for the pitfall of believing that you will become one happy family with two sets of children. Your children may not want to "blend," and by resisting may be communicating their need to retain boundaries, as discussed in Chapter 2.

- Have family meetings frequently, where each child can talk about feelings and can ask to have his or her needs met. Brainstorm ideas for each of your children to see that they get what they need, at least for part of the time, or at least in a modified way.

Watch out for the pitfall of believing that you will become one happy family with two sets of children.

- Because problems between stepchildren can become serious, issues that are not easily resolved should also be talked about with the coparent in the other home. Especially when children have stepsiblings in both of their homes, coparents have the responsibility to communicate about how their sons and daughters are doing.

Children and Sexuality

Though the subject of sexuality in the stepfamily can be difficult to talk about, this topic is important to address. We are all sexual beings, and this critical aspect of our existence makes the continuation of human life possible. Three concerns about sexuality emerge in second marriage families that I see:

- Sexuality and the stepcouple.
- Sexuality between stepsiblings.
- Sexuality between stepparent and stepchild.

Before children are born in original families, affection and sexuality are private aspects of the married couple's life. Children born into the family observe the degree of openness about physical touch and love displayed by their parents, and develop a level of comfort with its expression. Whether parents are demonstrative or more reserved about showing their feelings of love, the family develops a style of handling the parents' sexuality.

In second marriages with children, boys and girls are presented with new displays of affection between one of their parents and another adult. Discomfort often develops and the child's anxiety about sex usually increases. Because it is a normal response, this kind of reaction should be anticipated and expected by parents and stepparents as well. Children, especially older school-age children and teens, will almost always object to seeing the stepcouple show sexual or romantic affection.

To address the matter of your child's reaction to your style of displaying affection after remarriage, you should talk to your son or daughter about the subject, use the skill of reflective listening to learn how he or she feels, and adjust your romantic behavior in the home if necessary. You may need to compromise with a child who objects to seeing you kiss, for example, by agreeing just to hug in the presence of the children. Anxiety about sexuality that is not discussed can drive a child away, especially an adolescent with sexual urges. If your child or stepchild of any age is put off by your open affection, or if your child feels left out when you hold hands, cut down on how you show your love for each other openly in the home.

Anxiety about sexuality that is not discussed can drive a child away, especially an adolescent with sexual urges.

To deal with the concern about sexuality between stepchildren, set mandatory boundaries for them in the form of household rules. Children should be told, for example, not to touch each other's bodies, and perhaps should be limited to shaking hands or giving "high-fives" as gestures of affection. Stepsiblings are at risk for sexual experimentation because they do not have the natural sense of "hands off" that they had in the family of origin. Reacting to each other more like friends than family members, adolescents may feel sexual attraction, and many need their parents' help to ward off inappropriate behavior.

The matter of sexuality involving a stepparent and stepchild is perhaps the easiest to address, because it is illegal, entirely inappropriate, and harmful to the child. Stepfathers should maintain physical limits with their stepdaughters, since allegations about sexual contact are most frequently reported to authorities. Even mothers or daughters who trust a new step-father may misinterpret his affection and become suspicious about his behavior. Though a mother may find it distasteful to talk to her daughter about keeping healthy boundaries in interactions with her stepfather, a loving talk about what is appropriate and inappropriate might prevent an unnecessary family crisis from erupting.

Suggestions

- Talk with your new spouse about how sexuality and affection will be handled in your family, so each of you can be reassured that the children will be safe — emotionally as well as physically.

- Set limits for the children about touching each other, playing together physically, and about sleeping in separate rooms. Never have stepsiblings of the opposite sex share bedrooms, and set firm consequences for breaking these rules.

- Be open about talking about boundaries in your home. Bring up problems at regular family meetings, so secrets or feelings of shame or embarrassment do not go unattended.

- Talk to your coparent in the other home regarding how concerns about intimacy and affection are handled at your house. Keep in mind that trust between you and your child's other parent is the most important dynamic for continuing family happiness.

Issues with Extended Families

The emotional ramifications of divorce affect many family members other than mother, father, and children. Grandparents on both sides, brothers and sisters of the spouses, nieces and nephews, cousins, and close friends all mourn the loss of the family as they knew it. No matter how hard a separating mother and father may try to keep the problems between them, extended family will feel the effects.

Remarriage is a second chance at happiness for the bride and groom, and also a second chance for the children and extended family. Because of the sheer numbers of relatives and step-relatives that come into second families, though, dealing with so many personalities can be difficult. And because of the many problematic patterns that can develop between coparents, stepparents, and crossparents, stress and negative feelings about relatives outside either household can also emerge.

Parents and stepparents in second marriages should first counter the effects of grief and loss by making sure they keep ties with the child's original extended family intact. Because children's two-home families are at the center of importance to each of them, it follows that all their grandparents, aunts, uncles, and cousins are also valuable. Boys and girls who have gone through divorce derive a great sense of security from regular visits with relatives who are removed enough from the conflict to relax and enjoy time with them. After remarriage contact with step-aunts, uncles, cousins, and other step-relative counterparts is of secondary importance, but getting to know these new relatives at family functions can help in a similar way. Children have lost a lot by the time they get to the point of healing in a stepfamily, and being introduced to extended family members of a parent's new spouse counteracts some of the loss.

Boys and girls who have gone through divorce derive a great sense of security from regular visits with relatives who are removed enough from the conflict to relax and enjoy time with them.

In situations where members of the extended family or stepfamily are angry or hurt, or where they themselves cannot accept a family member, the challenge falls to the child's coparents and new stepparents to fight the urge to limit the child's world by leaving them out of the picture. Too often a child misses out on valuable family relationships because of bitterness between the adults who feel they are doing the right thing to "end" the conflict with estrangement. Loving parents do their children emotional favors with their efforts to stay in contact with extended family when they can.

Suggestions

- ◆ Use the skills of positive communication and good family manners in conversations with original and step-grandparents and in-laws. Even when relatives outside the immediate family are unreasonable, continue to be reasonable yourself, for the sake of controlling conflict.

- ◆ Develop traditions of maintaining contact with your children's extended family in addition to getting together for visits. Use cards to mark holidays and birthdays, and remember the value of regular phone calls. Make use of cell phones and email when you can, because these tools make contact easy.

- ◆ When serious conflict develops between a member of your household and a relative, try addressing the problem by asking a family member who is neutral to intervene on your behalf. Disengage for a while if you need to, but remember to make efforts to reunite when you can, for the well-being of the entire family.

It is outside the scope of this parenting guide for me to try to address every common problem that could develop in families of divorce and remarriage. The bulk of suggestions that I have offered apply mostly to families where the homes are fairly close to each other and where there is frequent contact between children and each of their parents. When large geographical distances separate the children's homes, there are sometimes fewer problems facing the network of parents because there is less need to work together on a day-to-day basis. In other cases long-distance parenting across two homes is very conflictual, such as when there is little trust between a child's two sets of parenting figures. When this is the case, parents and stepparents have a serious responsibility to stay flexible and communicate effectively so each child's parenting time can be free of conflict.

I encourage you to see that regardless of individual circumstances, most issues for most families can be resolved by being flexible and by being determined to talk and listen productively to each other, in person, by telephone or by email. In almost every case parents who are determined to be successful in working together can manage to adopt an attitude of optimism that serves them well. By applying the skills of positive problem-solving and by using coping techniques presented throughout this guide you, your spouse and the parents in your child's other home should be able work your way through conflict.

Not So Common Problems

Although situations that are very serious are rare, when they surface they must be addressed. When a coparent or stepparent has a significant mental illness, when there is domestic violence in the family, or when a parent has a serious substance abuse problem, special precautions must be taken to protect the children. Even in these situations, however, the three golden rules apply:

1. *Put the needs of the children first.*

2. *Respect the parenting chain of command.*

3. *Use your family manners.*

When one parent behaves erratically because of a chronic psychological condition, it is up to the other parent or parents to get outside help in setting up rules for contact between parent and child. Physical and psychological safety are fundamental necessities for every boy and girl. Beyond taking these precautions it is usually still the responsibility of the healthy parent to cope with problematic incidents or odd behavior compassionately and resist cutting off all contact. The child needs time with even a troubled parent, so long as it is safe, to develop a sense of identity.

One strategy for coping with a serious, chronic problem in another parent involves accepting the reality that your own gentle teachings to your child about the problem will make a great difference in the long run. For example, explaining serious depression as a condition that underlies a parent's habit of not showing up for a child's activities can help the child understand the parent's inconsistency. Or explaining that a child cannot sleep over at one parent's home because the father or mother is likely to get drunk and aggressive in the evening can help the child accept things as they are.

Your own gentle teachings to your child about the problem will make a great difference in the long run.

In families where the potential for domestic violence requires outside help, court orders may be necessary for years into a second marriage to prevent tragedy. Even when you need the safeguards of restraining orders and permanent supervision of a child's parenting time, however, your responsibility to respect the child's right to a relationship with that parent continues. Here the ongoing dialogue between parent, stepparent, and child is crucial for helping the child develop the best understanding of reality.

Several things are important to remember when parents have the job of living day-to-day in the face of a serious, ongoing problem. First, talk to your child and spouse frequently about the parent in question. Without passing judgement on him or her as a person, communicate honestly with everyone involved about how the child can maintain a safe relationship with that parent. When you have dealt with this important responsibility, shift your attention to more pleasant times with your stepfamily and concentrate on fun and happiness, so you all experience well-being in other areas of your lives. Cope with the ongoing stress by opting out of arguments and confrontations whenever you can, so your everyday life can be manageable.

Regrouping After Regression

Regression occurs when pressure causes a child or adult to revert to an earlier stage of maturity in how they cope with anxiety. For example, the temper tantrums commonly displayed by two-year-olds often reappear in twelve-year-olds as they are faced with the demands of adolescence. In parents who have gone through separation, the level of conflict usually seen right after divorce can resurface when one or both of them react to the complications of remarriage. Problems between coparents adjusting to family changes are often poorly resolved during this period of transition because they regress in their ability to work together. To a considerable extent this dynamic is a natural response to stress, and it should almost be expected to happen.

As I illustrated in Chapter 3, the number of relationships in the family parental system increases dramatically after remarriage, making regression in communication almost inevitable. The hassles of everyday life with children are great enough by themselves, and when there are three or four parents involved they can become overwhelming. No wonder even the most dedicated of parents become impatient, cave in, and react unsuccessfully when they are faced with so much stress.

Because the needs of the children come first, parents, stepparents, and crossparents who find themselves slipping backward in how they cope have a responsibility to stop the regression. The first member of the parenting team to notice that home-to-home relationships are deteriorating should alert the others to the need to regroup and regain maturity. Call in-home or between-home meetings if you have to, and reactivate all the strategies you have learned. Red flags of escalating arguments, disagreements, and misunderstandings should never go unheeded. For the sake of the children in both homes, coparents and their spouses should always strive to do better in how they deal with each other.

Call in-home or between-home meetings if you have to, and reactivate all the strategies you have learned.

Laying the Groundwork for Gratitude

In the end there is only one reason why parents of divorce and remarriage should put so much effort into the family. This is simply for the well-being of the children you have loved since birth and who you will love forever. Your worry about them is your source of motivation to do a good job in parenting, and your sense of the future should be your ongoing guide.

Children never choose to be born, but as they grow and mature they become grateful for their mothers' and fathers' hard work in raising them. Older children and teens develop insight about pressures of the world, and they learn to acknowledge the hardships faced by their parents. Young adults whose parents stayed together gain appreciation for the effort it took to resist temptations to split, and those whose parents went through divorce come to understand why it happened.

Most modern day parents truly hope that the national divorce rate which has now leveled off — will drop more dramatically in our children's generation. Not wanting our sons and daughters to suffer the pain of loss that we suffered, we hope they will do better. We want our children to have relationships that last, and we want them to be optimistic about values like trust between men and women.

In this book I have set forth ideas to show parents that families can stabilize after separation, even in the face of complexities. Now your job is to activiate the strategies and do the very best you can right now, so your children will be able to thank you when they are older.

~~~~~~~~~~~~~~~~~~~~~~~~~~~~~~~~

Afterward

THE CHILD LOOKING BACK

Fast-forward your imaginary video camera twenty years from now and record this scene with your child and his friend. Grown, and with a spouse of his own, the young man is smiling, animated, and enjoying the conversation. This is what you see and hear:

"Yes, my parents divorced when I was eight. I remember being sad at first, and wishing they'd get back together. It was really very painful, and the worst part was the fighting. But you'll never guess what happened! After a little while, Mom and Dad learned to get along better, and I think they even liked each other more. I really remember feeling relieved, and I learned to be a kid again.

"Then both of them remarried, and I got another shock! Two weddings in one year, and a world of new stuff to deal with. But I have to give Mom and Dad credit – both of them always put us kids first and were concerned about how we felt. Within a short time I discovered I now had four parents caring about me. It was weird, but I was happy, and life has been good ever since.

"I don't really like divorce, and I don't think either one of my parents did either. But they and my stepparents did an awesome job of getting along for the sake of all their children. I will love them all forever."

Although life doesn't have a finish line, a scene like this for your child should be the goal for all parents and stepparents, whether separated, divorced, living together, or remarried.

References

Ahrons, Constance. *We're Still Family: What Grown Children Have to Say About Their Parents' Divorce.* New York: Harper Collins, 2004.

Baris, M.A.; Coates; C.A., Duvall, B.B.; Garrity, C.B.; Johnson, E.T.; and LaCross, E.R.. *Working with High-Conflict Families of Divorce: A Guide for Professionals.* New Jersey: Jason Aronson, Inc., Northvale, 2001.

Bray, James H. and Kelly, John. *Stepfamilies: Love, Marriage, and Parenting in the First Decade,* New York: Broadway Books, 1998.

Carnegie, Dale. *How to Win Friends and Influence People,* 1936.

Clapp, Genevieve. *Divorce and New Beginnings.* New York: John Wiley & Sons, 2000.

Coates, Christine A. and LaCrosse, Robert E.. *Learning From Divorce: How to Take Responsibility, Stop the Blame and Move On.* San Francisco, California: Jossey-Bass, 2003.

Fisher, Bruce. *When Your Relationship Ends.,* San Luis Obispo, California: Impact Publishers, 1981.

Fitzgerald, Helen. *The Grieving Child, A Parent's Guide.* New York: Fireside, 1992.

Garrity, Carla B. and Baris, Mitchell A. *Caught in the Middle.* Lexington Books, 1994.

Goleman, Daniel. *Emotional Intelligence.* New York: Bantam Books, 1994.

Gottman, John, with Declare, Joan. *Raising an Emotionally Intelligent Child.* New York: Fireside, 1997.

Gottman, John M. and Silver, Nan. *The Seven Principles for Making Marriage Work,* New York: Three Rivers Press, 1999.

Gottman, Jonathan W.; Notarius, Cliff,; Gonso, Jonni,; and Markman, Howard., *A Couple's Guide to Communication.* Champaign, Illinois: Research Press, 1976.

Hetherington, E. Mavis and Kelly, John. *For Better or for Worse.* New York: W.W. Norton & Company, 2002.

Hoffman, Martin L.. *Empathy and Moral Development: Implications for Caring and Justice.* New York: Cambridge University Press, 2000.

Kübler-Ross, Elisabeth. *On Death and Dying.* New York: MacMillan, 1969.

Levy, David. *The Best Parent is Both Parents: A Guide to Shared Parenting in the 21st Century.* Norfolk, Virginia: Hampton Rhodes, 1993.

McBride, Jean. *Encouraging Words for New Stepmothers*. Fort Collins, Colorado: CDR Press, 2001.

Myers, David G. *The Pursuit of Happiness*. New York: Harper Collins, 1992.

Pruett, Kyle D. Fatherneed. *Why Father Care is as Essential as Mother Care for Your Child*. New York: The Free Press, 2000.

Ricci, Isolina, *Mom's House, Dad's House: Making Two Homes for Your Child*. New York: The Free Press, 2000.

Thomas, Shirley. *Parents Are Forever: A Step-by-Step Guide to Becoming Successful Coparents After Divorce: Revised Edition*. Longmont, Colorado: Springboard Publications, 2004.

Visher, Emily B. and Visher, John S. *How to Win as a Stepfamily*. New York: Brunner/Mazel, 1982.

Wallerstein, Judith S.; Lewis, Julia M.; and Blakeslee, Sandra. *The Unexpected Legacy of Divorce*. New York: Hyperion, 2000.

Wallerstein, Judith S. and Blakeslee, Sandra, *Second Chances: Men, Women and Children a Decade After Divorce, Who Wins, Who Loses and Why*. New York: Ticknor & Fields, 1990.

Warshak, Richard A. *Divorce Poison*. New York: Regan Books, 2001.

Resources for Parents

Center for Divorce Education
A nonprofit organization founded in 1987 to educate the
public, distribute information about divorce and it's effects
on children, and promote effective education programs for
parents and children that minimize the harmful effects of
divorce. www.divorce-education.com

Parents Are Forever
Dr. Thomas' site offering advice and direction to parents and
children of divorce. View *Parents Are Forever: A Step-by-Step
Guide to Becoming Successful Coparents After Divorce* (2004) and
*Divorced But Still My Parents: A Helping-Book About Divorce for
Children and Parents* (1997). www.parentsareforever.com

Our Family Wizard
Provides life management tools designed to help families
with scheduling and managing important family information.
Allows families to quickly store and access information from
anywhere in the world. www.ourfamilywizard.com

Family Works, Inc.
Features the innovative Parenting Wisely interactive parent
skills training program shown by research evidence to
improve parents' effectiveness with teens, pre-teens, and
young children. Training available online.
www.parentingwisely.com

Solutions for Families
A private organization dedicated to offering solution-focused
services for families of divorce. Excellent resource for
professionals looking for training on divorce education and
for bringing comprehensive services to their communities.
www.solutions4families.com

Up to Parents
Free interactive site offering parents who register to receive
personalized help with shielding their children from the
harmful effects of divorce. www.uptoparents.org

Stepfamily Association of America
National nonprofit membership organization dedicated
to successful stepfamily living. Provides educational
information and resources for anyone interested in
stepfamilies and their issues. www.saafamilies.org

Stepfamily Foundation
Mission is to assist parents to make the family work as
it is now. Offers telephone counseling, seminars for
professionals, and lectures worldwide. www.stepfamily.org